HOW TO WORK WITH AN
ARCHITECT

HOW TO WORK WITH AN
ARCHITECT

GERALD LEE MOROSCO, AIA
PHOTOGRAPHS BY ED MASSERY

Gibbs Smith, Publisher
Salt Lake City

First Edition
10 09 08 07 06   5 4 3 2

Published by
Gibbs Smith, Publisher
P.O. Box 667
Layton, Utah 84041

Orders: 1.800.748.5439
www.gibbs-smith.com

Designed by Pamela Beverly-Quigley, Boulder, CO
Printed and bound in Hong Kong

Library of Congress Cataloging-in-Publication Data

Morosco, Gerald Lee.
How to work with an architect / Gerald Lee
Morosco ; photography by Ed Massery.— 1st ed.
    p. cm.
  ISBN 1-4236-0007-X
 1. Architects and patrons. 2. Architect-designed
houses. 3. Architecture, Domestic—Planning.
I. Massery, Edward R. II. Title.

NA7115.M67 2006
728'.37—dc22

2005033876

For the Taliesin Fellowship, where I came to appreciate the value of maintaining a beautiful environment in which to live and work and first came to understand the essential importance of cultivating and sustaining an effective working relationship with one's clients. And with my appreciation to John Milnes Baker, AIA, whose original book, *How to Build a House with an Architect,* has informed clients over two decades of my professional practice and inspired this writing.

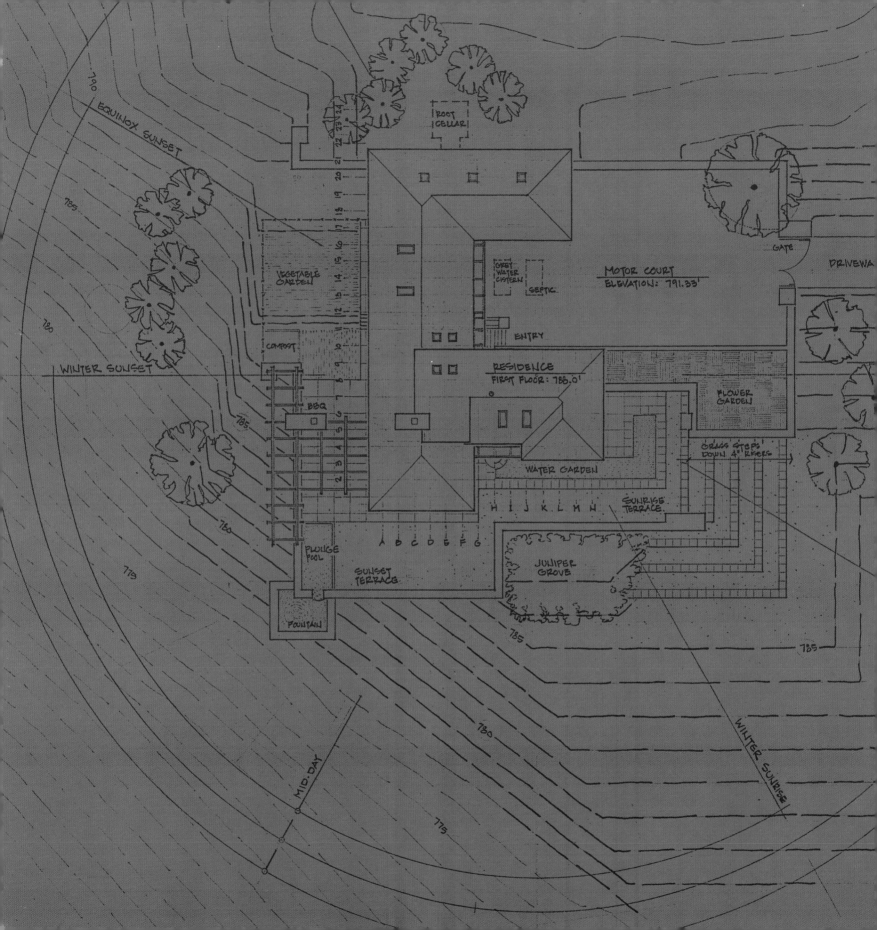

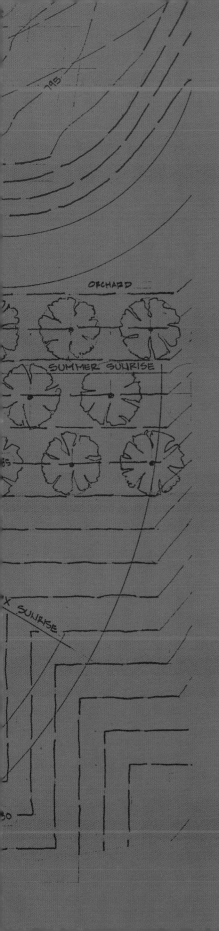

Contents

Acknowledgements

The content of this book draws upon the well-spring of relationships that I have cultivated with scores of residential clients over almost three decades of professional practice. The idea for the book grew out of a series of informal discussion groups that I have moderated annually for more than a decade at the Grove Park Inn Arts and Crafts Conference in Asheville, North Carolina. These discussion groups have focused on how to effectively work with an architect, and I thank Bruce Johnson, conference director, for continuing to afford me the opportunity to participate.

Following one such group three years ago, Christopher Robbins, general manager of Gibbs Smith, Publisher, lingered to inquire about my interest in writing a book on the subject of working with an architect. His enthusiasm for the project was exceeded only by his tenacity. This writing is the result of his indefatigable confidence in the potential for the book and the support of all at Gibbs Smith, Publisher.

Encouraging, advising, and cajoling me from the first draft through to the final rewrites has been my dear friend Judith Kelly, who persevered in everything from searching out permissions to writing many of the sidebars. I quite simply could not have accomplished the writing of this book while simultaneously maintaining my architectural practice without her valuable assistance.

Thanks are also in order to my many current clients and their contractors, who were patient when deadlines for this book project made me sometimes unavailable to attend immediately to them. And to several potential clients, patiently awaiting my attentions, who will now have the benefit of this book as a preface to our work together.

My trusted and loyal staff—Lora Samuelson, Suzanne Tush, Nathan Werner, Bryan David Henne, and Drew Bercini—have been most forgiving and accommodating. Collectively, they kept the home fires burning while also helping with the production of this book. Beyond maintaining the work of our office, Drew, Bryan, and Nathan were variously responsible for the organization, delineation and production of the graphic images and illustrations used in the book.

I also acknowledge Peter Rött, AIA, and Fred Fargotstein, RA, who both worked for many years as associates in my practice. Their contributions are directly evidenced throughout the book in various drawings and also by way of their work in helping to develop and see through to construction many of the actual projects.

The careful photographic images of my work herein benefit from my fifteen-year collaboration with gifted architectural-photographer Ed Massery. For the majority of the depicted projects, he was ably assisted by Patrick Buerkle.

I would like to thank my several clients who provided us access to photograph their homes and have allowed me to include the images in this book: Toni Ault, Pam and R. F. Culbertson, Kathy and Bob Dryburgh, Martha Fleming, Kathy and Ed Friedman, Beverly and Harry Friedman, Marla Gendleman and Harvey Block, Marsha and Bernie Marcus, Michelle Pilecki and Tom Clinton, Barbara and Ernie Thrasher, and Rena and Ed Wing.

In addition to my own work with clients, I have drawn on the collective experiences of the architectural profession documented in the publications of the American Institute of Architects and its constituent chapters, and the California Architects Board and its Landscape Architects Technical Committee. My thanks to Cassandra Brown of AIA National; Pamela de Oliveira-Smith of the Boston Society of Architects/AIA; Camille Victour and Mary Fierle of AIA Asheville; Sue Martin and Coleen Galvan of the California Architects Board; and Mona Maggio and Justin Sotelo of the California Landscape Architects Technical Committee for their kind assistance in securing permissions to adapt and incorporate portions of their publications or Web sites.

This writing indeed benefits from the perspectives of others who have afforded the use of their own words, as well as from the words and insights of many historical architects.

Many have also supported this endeavor with their input, advice, and review of the manuscript: Caroline Boyce of AIA Pennsylvania; Anne Swager of AIA Pittsburgh; Beverly Hart; Val M. Cox; Tara Merenda of the Community Design Center; Catherine McCollom; Pamela Golden; Constance Nelson; Mary Navarro; Marion Monheim; Dr. Marsha Marcus; Indira Berndtson of the Frank Lloyd Wright Archives; Bryan Henne; Paul Ford; Lora Samuelson; Ed Massery; my mother, Phyllis Morosco; and my sister and client, Jane Elizabeth Haines.

I am indebted to Aimee Stoddard, my editor at Gibbs Smith, Publisher. Kind and patient in her professional judgment of this, my first book, she encouraged me throughout.

Lastly, I owe my heartfelt and deepest thanks to Paul Ford, whose love and support has buoyed my sometimes flagging spirits and sustained me through all and everything.

Gerald Lee Morosco
Pittsburgh, Pennsylvania

View of porch addition appropriate to the historic character of this house designed in 1929 by Alden & Harlow, the inheritors of the architectural practice of Henry Hobson Richardson. Richardson was one of America's most important early architects.

Introduction

"A loving atmosphere in your home is the foundation for your life. . . . Do all you can to create a tranquil, harmonious home."

—From a Nepalese good luck mantra

My interest in architecture is tied to my earliest memories. My beloved great-aunt Mary Jane Marasco recalled my declared intention to become an architect at age two. Regardless of the veracity of her recollection, scrapbooks from my childhood abound with increasingly detailed building drawings. Photo albums evidence the long summer days I spent on the shores of Lake Erie constructing elaborately conceived sand castles.

At midpoint on the newspaper delivery route I attended to for several years, there was an architect who maintained a small practice in the back of his house. In good weather, I would hail him through the screen door, and he would oblige me with a short visit. I would sit for a few mesmerizing minutes on a tall stool beside his drafting table and observe the precise gestures of his pencil along his T-square and triangle.

During my college years, my interest in the work of Frank Lloyd Wright took root. In the summer before my senior year, I worked in northern Arizona as a laborer on the construction of a utopian city project called Arcosanti that was conceived by former Frank Lloyd Wright apprentice Paolo Soleri. One weekend, I hitchhiked seventy miles south to Phoenix to Wright's desert outpost, Taliesin West.

It was there I discovered that the fellowship established in 1932 by Wright and his wife, Olgivanna, was flourishing under her direction, together with the architectural firm that succeeded Wright's own practice upon his death in 1959. When I discovered that it was still possible to apprentice at Taliesin, I dismissed my

Driveway entry view of the porch addition to the Alden & Harlow house.

previous plan to pursue postgraduate education in favor of an apprenticeship there.

After meeting Mrs. Wright for an interview the following January, she accepted me as an apprentice in the Taliesin Fellowship. Two weeks following my graduation from college, I found my way to Spring Green, Wisconsin, where the fellowship continued to spend its summers at Wright's original Taliesin estate.

At Taliesin, I lived and worked communally with many who had lived and worked directly with Frank Lloyd Wright. We followed an educational model based on learning by doing. I was thrust immediately into the drafting studio, where I learned the art and craft of architecture by working on real projects that necessitated direct communication and contact with clients. By way of experiences over the course of my five-year apprenticeship, I came to understand my vocation not in the abstract sense, which is the inherent drawback of a conventional academic education,

but in terms of the connection between a client's needs, wants, dreams, and budget. And, I learned the architect's responsibility to translate those sometimes intangible factors into a three-dimensional reality of utility and beauty.

In my first year at Taliesin, I visited a local bookstore, where I came upon a copy of *How to Build a House with an Architect,* by John Milnes Baker, AIA. I was attracted to the book by Baker's drawings, which were rendered somewhat in Wright's style. Beyond the illustrations, however, Baker's thoughtful narrative was my first lesson in the often misunderstood, and sometimes disastrously uninformed, relationship between residential clients and their architects.

Most clients approach an architect with no prior experience or understanding of the complex process involved in building or remodeling a home, let alone the somewhat mysterious roles and responsibilities of the respective parties. Unfortunately, many architects approach the situation as business as usual, neglecting to take the time to carefully describe the process to their clients at the outset.

As a young man in architecture, I understood the importance of a well-informed and mutually communicative architect-client relationship. I have passed along dozens of copies of Baker's primer to scores of my clients over the past twenty years as required reading prior to beginning our work together. I have given a copy to every young architect-in-training I have mentored as well.

A casual Internet Google search for the phrase *how to work with an architect* yields more than thirty-six million hits. With effort, you can cull through that number to identify several hundred that might actually reveal useful information on the topic. However, it is currently impossible for someone interested in working with an architect to find a single comprehensive guide on the Internet or in print that explains how to establish and maintain the client-architect relationship in order to successfully complete a project.

I have authored *How to Work with an Architect,* in part, to replace my dog-eared copies of Baker's long-out-of-print book. Mostly, though, I hope to pass along my understanding gained through more than two decades of work in residential architecture. Key to that understanding is my observation that working with an architect is, at its essence, a very personal relationship, even though a contract, establishing terms for remuneration in exchange for professional services, renders it a business transaction. Acknowledging and welcoming the profoundly personal nature of the association places both parties in a position to derive the greatest benefit, value, and enjoyment from the process.

In my first meetings with prospective clients, I use the analogy of personal relationships to make the process of selecting and working with an architect more understandable. I characterize the initial meeting as the "first date." This date may be "blind"—set up by friends of the client who themselves may have had a prior relationship with the architect—set up as the result of a client's Internet query or search of the telephone directory, or it may have come about as a result of some previous direct introduction. Regardless, both parties approach this first date as do many couples, with nothing but the highest mutual expectations for success.

Views of kitchen remodelings of three early-twentieth-century houses reflect the distinctive style of each.

Introduction

Continuity of materials in the author's modest row house contributes to a sense of greater space.

If the date is a success, it will be, perhaps, followed by another, after which the client and architect will commit to a relationship. The singular goal of the relationship will be the conception of a design for a new home or for alterations to an existing dwelling.

The conception is the fun part of the process. Nothing is as exciting and stimulating as the creation of a new form out of the combination of the client's requirements and the architect's vision. Following the conception, the design

must be brought to term over a protracted period of growth and development during which the design concept takes form. In the entire relationship, the hardest part is the labor, at which time the contractor is introduced into the mix and delivers that which client and architect have conceived.

I typically suggest to my clients that, as with childbirth, the pain of labor one experiences is often forgotten after becoming caught up in the joy of what has been delivered. And, not infrequently, people choose to undertake the whole design process again. In one meeting I had with prospective clients, the wife advised me that she had given birth three times via cesarean section and wondered if such an option existed for the construction of their home!

The process of conceiving a custom design solution for your home with an architect can be one of the most remarkable, memorable, and lasting endeavors of your life.

Author's color pencil rendering of an initial design concept for a kitchen addition to an existing Arts and Crafts–style house.

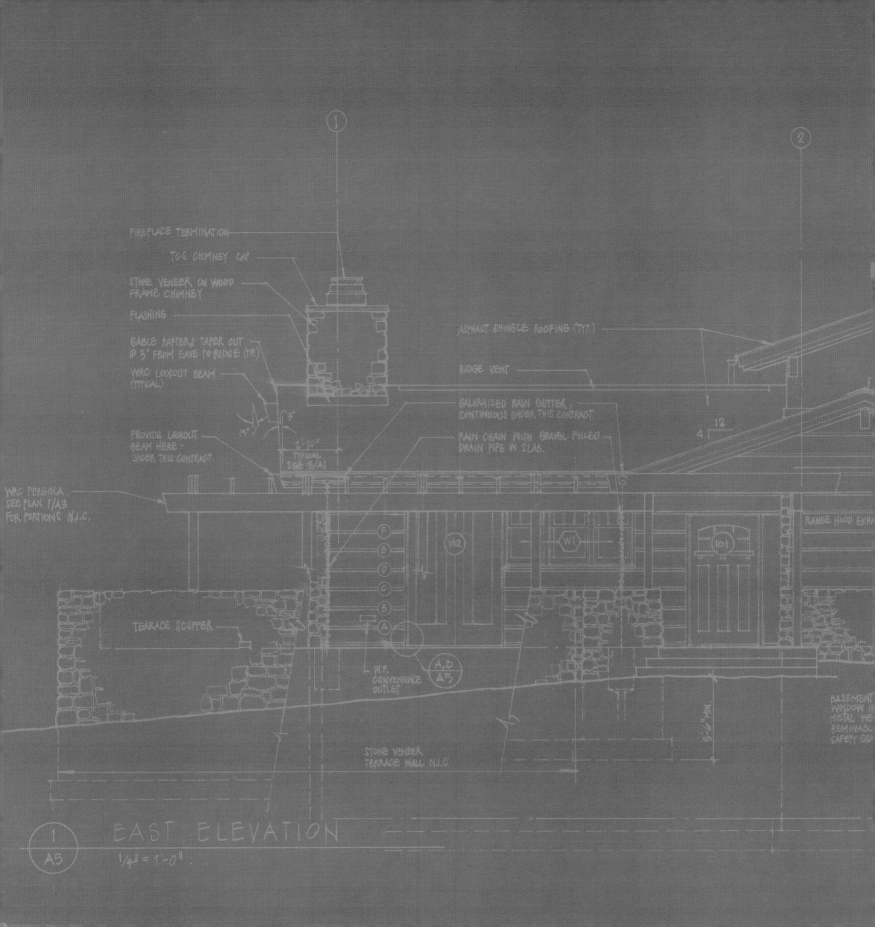

FIREPLACE TERMINATION

TGS CHIMNEY CAP

STONE VENEER ON WOOD
FRAME CHIMNEY

FLASHING

GABLE RAFTERS TAPER OUT
@ 3" FROM EAVE TO RIDGE (TYP.)

WRC LOOKOUT BEAM
(TYPICAL)

PROVIDE LOOKOUT
BEAM HERE -
UNDER THIS CONTRACT.

WRC PERGOLA.
SEE PLAN 1/A3
FOR PORTIONS N.I.C.

TERRACE SCUPPER

ASPHALT SHINGLE ROOFING (TYP.)

RIDGE VENT

GALVANIZED RAIN GUTTER,
CONTINUOUS UNDER THIS CONTRACT.

RAIN CHAIN WITH GRAVEL FILLED
DRAIN PIPE IN SLAB.

RANGE HOOD EXHA

W.P.
CONVENIENCE
OUTLET

STONE VENEER
TERRACE WALL N.I.C.

BASEMENT
WINDOW
METAL W6
REMOVABL
SAFETY GR

EAST ELEVATION

1/4" = 1'-0"

Part I

DO YOU REALLY NEED AN
Architect?

Hearth and home—a most endearing example
of the enduring Craftsman bungalow.

Architect

"What is and who is an architect, and how and why is he? . . . Well, the word arch, *in the sense that it's in architecture, means like the archbishop, means the top, the arch, the high one, the one above all the others. Then* tech *of course you know the meaning of; that's technology, technique,* tech *like the Toltecs.* Tech *means the know-how, means how to put things together. So the proper translation of the word* architect *is the 'master of the know-how.' "*

—Frank Lloyd Wright speaking to the Taliesin Fellowship, November 30, 1958

The Title of Architect

Architect is a designation, like doctor or lawyer, reserved by law for those who are licensed by their respective state boards to engage in professional practice. Licensing is required by all states. However, statutes vary, with some being so restrictive as to actually prohibit architects registered in one state from offering their services in any other before obtaining registration in that state. Such statutes have been established to protect the health, safety, and welfare of the public from non-registrants who have not met the requisite educational requirements nor demonstrated the required competencies for professional licensure.

You can inquire about the registration status of an architect through any state's board of registration. State boards can also advise you of any disciplinary action they have taken against a particular architect.

Architect Licensing Requirements

All states require individuals to successfully complete the Architect Registration Examination (ARE), which is administered by the National Council of Architectural Registration Boards (NCARB), before a license can be issued.

Architects are examined for competence in the following areas:

- Knowledge of applicable building and zoning codes, structural regulations, and governmental review processes required by the state in which they are seeking a license.
- Ability to evaluate and advise on issues relating to property acquisition, infrastructure requirements, zoning, construction regulations, and other areas where architects' experience and recommendations are valuable to clients.
- Ability to develop project plans; prepare planning, schematic, and preliminary studies; and prepare designs, working drawings, and specifications.
- Ability to coordinate services and/or preparation of documents by technical and special consultants, such as land surveyors and professional engineers.
- Ability to provide technical assistance in the preparation of bid documents and agreements between clients and contractors.
- Ability to administer the contract—in other words, to fully provide the services detailed in the agreement between the architect and client.
- Ability to provide oversight and observation during the construction phase of the project.

States differ in their criteria for candidates to become eligible to take the examinations, and also in the type and number of exams required. Historically, architects became eligible to take their licensing examinations by way of apprenticeship (traditionally taking twelve years following the completion of high school) or through some combination of traditional education and apprenticeship. Many registered architects practicing today, this author included, do not hold degrees in architecture.

In the mid-1980s, seeking to establish uniformity in licensure and to assure a steady flow of students into accredited college, university, and professional schools of architecture, the National Architectural Accrediting Board (NAAB) successfully lobbied most state legislatures to amend their licensure laws to establish an NAAB-accredited degree as prerequisite for the registration examinations. For this reason, the Frank Lloyd Wright School of Architecture transitioned its long-standing apprenticeship program at Taliesin into an NAAB-accredited degree program.

Most states today require that a candidate have a minimum of five years of professional schooling, culminating in an NAAB-accredited degree, and three years of work experience in the offices of registered architects before he or she is eligible to take the licensing examinations.

View from the living room of the Craftsman bungalow looking through to the dining cove.

Only licensed architects may use the title *architect*, and the drawings prepared under their direction must bear the architect's seal. For this reason, it is not uncommon for architects to follow their name with the words *registered architect* or *RA*. Some architects join the American Institute of Architects and use the appellation *AIA*. Many architects also maintain certification with the National Council of Architectural Registration Boards (NCARB) and may use this appellation in lieu of, or in addition to, the others. Certification with NCARB signifies that the architect maintains a license to practice architecture in at least one state. Depending on the particulars of his or her original registration, an architect may use NCARB certification to facilitate reciprocal registration between states. As in other licensed professions, architects are required to renew their registration periodically (typically every two years).

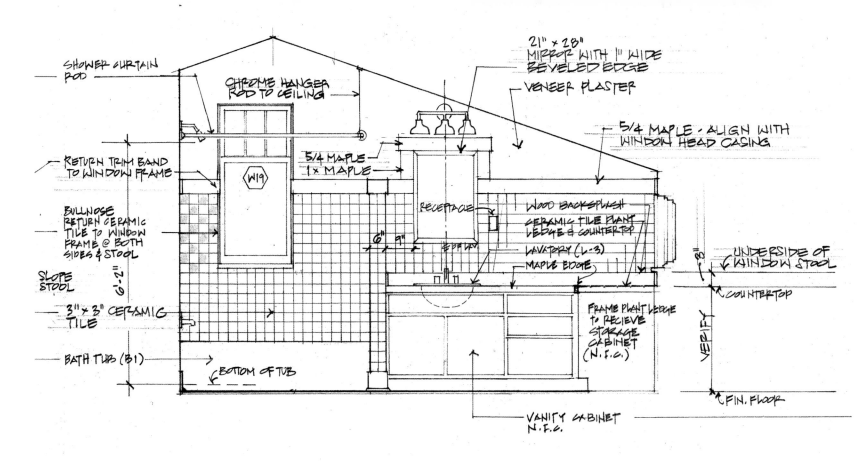

The labels on the drawing include:

SHOWER CURTAIN ROD

CHROME HANGER ROD TO CEILING

21" x 28" MIRROR WITH 1" WIDE BEVELED EDGE

VENEER PLASTER

5/4 MAPLE - ALIGN WITH WINDOW HEAD CASING

RETURN TRIM BAND TO WINDOW FRAME

5/4 MAPLE 1x MAPLE

W19

BULLNOSE RETURN CERAMIC TILE TO WINDOW FRAME @ BOTH SIDES & STOOL

RECEPTACLE

WOOD BACKSPLASH
CERAMIC TILE PLANT LEDGE & COUNTERTOP

SLOPE STOOL

6'-2"

6" 9"

4" DEEP

LAVATORY (L-3)

MAPLE EDGE

UNDERSIDE OF WINDOW STOOL

3" x 3" CERAMIC TILE

COUNTERTOP

VERIFY

FRAME PLANT LEDGE TO RECIEVE STORAGE CABINET (N.I.C.)

BATH TUB (B1)

BOTTOM OF TUB

VANITY CABINET N.I.C.

FIN. FLOOR

An interior elevation drawing of the Craftsman bungalow guest bathroom from the construction documents.

Other Professionals

There are other design professionals and non-professionals who, depending on the jurisdiction, may offer design services in connection with single-family residential projects. Persons who do not have the education and training required to become architects will sometimes identify themselves as designers or architectural designers to avoid misrepresentation as registered architects. Some jurisdictions use the designations *architect-in-training* or *intern architect* to identify those who have met the educational and training requirements for licensure but have yet to complete registration examinations.

There is a movement among interior designers to distinguish themselves from interior *decorators* through licensure. As a result, many states now have education and training requirements and licensure examinations that are required to use the title *interior designer*. According to the American Society of Interior Designers, the following jurisdictions, as of 2005, impose some regulation on interior design: Alabama, Arkansas, California, Connecticut, District of Columbia, Florida, Georgia, Illinois, Kentucky, Louisiana, Maine, Maryland, Michigan, Minnesota, Missouri, Nevada, New Jersey, New Mexico, New York, Puerto Rico, Tennessee, Texas, Virginia, and Wisconsin.

A view of the completed Craftsman bungalow guest bathroom.

Also in the mix are the various credentials of increasingly competitive subspecialties, such as Certified Kitchen Designer (CKD) and Certified Kitchen and Bath Designer (CKBD). Most of the professionals who have these sub-specialty accreditations work in conjunction with kitchen and bath showrooms or at major home centers, such as Lowe's and Home Depot.

I mention these other design professionals and nonprofessionals because they are sometimes misconstrued as alternatives to working with an architect. I am confident that the informed decision to work with an architect will ulti-mately ensure that you achieve the more satis-factory result. An architect's unique set of skills and abilities will add tangible and lasting value to your project.

National Council of Architectural Registration Boards

The National Council of Architectural Registration Boards (NCARB) is one of five principal organizations in the United States that deals with the practice of architecture. (The others are the American Institute of Architects, the Association of Collegiate Schools of Architecture, National Architectural Accrediting Board, and the American Institute of Architectural Students.)

NCARB members are the architectural registration boards of the fifty states, the District of Columbia, and four U.S. territories. Each registration board has state-appointed architect and public members as well as administrators.

The mission of NCARB is evident in these two equally important goals: to work together as a council of member boards to safeguard the health, safety, and welfare of the public; and to assist member boards in carrying out their duties.

NCARB provides the following services: develops and recommends standards to be required of an applicant for architectural registration, develops and recommends standards regulating the practice of architecture, provides a process to member boards for certifying the qualifications of an architect for registration, and represents the interests of member boards before public and private agencies.

Adapted with permission by NCARB, 1801 K Street, NW, Suite 1100-K, Washington, DC, 20006.

Meaning behind the Monikers

AIA: Acronym for American Institute of Architects. Use of this designation implies that the user is a registered architect. However, as this acronym designates membership in an organization, misapplications are not regulated by state governments.

AIT: Acronym for Architect-in-Training. Used in some states to indicate that an individual has completed the requisite educational requirements and portions of the Architectural Registration Examinations but is not yet registered to practice as an architect.

Architect: Professional designation, usually established by law, for a person or firm professionally qualified and duly licensed to perform architectural services in a given state.

ASLA: Acronym for American Society of Landscape Architects. The user is a graduate of an accredited or society-registered landscape architecture program and/or is licensed to practice landscape architecture and has three or more years of experience.

CSI: Acronym for Construction Specifications Institute, a technical society that includes architects, engineers, constructors, specifiers, suppliers of construction products, building owners, and facilities managers. Registered architects use this acronym after RA or AIA.

Decorator or Interior Decorator: An unregulated, nonprofessional designation with meaning such that it may imply. Used interchangeably with the title *Interior Designer* in those jurisdictions where Interior Designers remain unregulated.

FAIA: Acronym for Fellow of the American Institute of Architects. Used in lieu of AIA, the acronym indicates the user has been elected by his or her peers to the College of Fellows of the AIA. The individual is recognized as an honored and experienced member of the profession.

Interior Designer: Increasingly used as a designation by law for a person or firm qualified and duly licensed to perform interior design services.

NCARB: Acronym for National Council of Architectural Registration Boards. User is registered with NCARB, which indicates that he or she is licensed to practice architecture in at least one jurisdiction in the United States. Depending on the basis for his or her initial registration, the architect may qualify for reciprocal registration in all states.

RA: Acronym for Registered Architect.

Registered Architect: Designation that is synonymous with the title of architect. Used only by licensed professionals.

RLA: Acronym for Registered Landscape Architect. A professional designation, usually by law, for a person or firm professionally qualified and duly licensed to perform landscape architectural services.

SARA: Acronym for the Society of American Registered Architects. Founded in 1956, SARA is a professional society whose membership is open to registered or licensed architects in any state.

TF: Acronym for Taliesin Fellow. Designates that the user was an apprentice at Taliesin between 1932 and 1986, is a current or former member of the Taliesin Fellowship at Taliesin from 1932 to present, or after 1986 is a graduate of the accredited degree program of the Frank Lloyd Wright School of Architecture. If used, this acronym appears after RA or AIA for registered architects.

A modified cruciform in plan, the north side of this Craftsman bungalow nestles firmly into the hillside. The southern exposure is left open to capture the sun and warm the house.

Should You Hire an Architect?

Once you understand just what the word *architect* connotes, the logical question to ask yourself is why it is necessary to work with one. This is usually a personal decision.

Every building project does not require a licensed architect's services, although requirements vary widely from jurisdiction to jurisdiction. Current California law, for example, provides that "persons who are not licensed as architects . . . can design . . . single-family dwellings of woodframe construction that are not more than two stories and basement in height."[1] In most states, as a matter of right, individuals may design and build their own homes, subject to applicable building ordinances and regulations.

There is one external requirement, however, that would necessitate the involvement of an architect in your project: the governing authorities in the location where you plan to build may require that the plans submitted for your project be prepared by a licensed architect. Aside from any such mandated relationship, my introductory experiences with clients have revealed their initial query to be more succinctly phrased as, "Do I really *want* an architect?" The answer to this fundamental question is best revealed by a discussion of exactly what an architect does.

[1] California Architects Board, *Consumer's Guide to Hiring an Architect*, 2000, 2–3.

The Magic Act of Design

An architect crafts your individual functional requirements, wants, and wishes; the conditions of your particular site or existing dwelling; your available funds; and the requirements of your schedule into a three-dimensional expression you will come to call home. At best, such acts render compositions of intrinsic beauty and economy that achieve a close harmony with the existing conditions of a site or a pre-existing structure.

This act of design remains an elusive and intangible process that is beyond most laypersons' desire to understand. I have come to regard the unique ability of architects to create visible forms out of a client's abstract ideas (and, in the case of couples, sometimes conflicting ideas) to be their greatest skill.

Nevertheless, the essential act of design, although arguably the most valuable and glamorous component of architects' services, actually represents only a small portion of the total services they customarily provide.

Evaluation of Existing Homes and Building Sites

Prior to any design work, an architect can offer you a careful and studied evaluation of your requirements, budget, and building site, each in terms of the other. In the case of an addition or remodel, an architect can assess the existing conditions of your present home. On many

HOUSE FOR MARTHA E. FLEMING
BUTLER COUNTY PENNSYLVANIA
GERALD LEE MOROSCO ARCHITECTS, P.C.
27 AUGUST 1996
©1996

The author's original Schematic Design presentation drawing accurately depicts the completed Craftsman bungalow project.

occasions, for example, I have been called to an initial meeting with prospective clients to discuss their plans for an addition to their home only to recognize that a simpler and less costly remodeling of the existing home's interior spaces would address their needs satisfactorily. Or, even more simply, that a careful rearrangement of their furniture would suffice. My office manager of fifteen years, Lora Samuleson, accuses me of talking more clients out of projects than we actually undertake.

Many lenders and some jurisdictions now require a certified home inspection as a condition of sale. Although an inspection can identify obvious structural or mechanical deficiencies, an architect can weigh in with professional observations as to the feasibility and cost of the functional alterations as well as remedies for the deficiencies identified by the home inspection. Most practicing architects maintain relationships with qualified contractors in all of the building trades and can call upon these

The Craftsman bungalow dining cove affords
a view of the woodland meadow beyond.

**Interior and exterior views of the
Craftsman bungalow kitchen.**

individuals to carry out more studied evaluations and prepare detailed cost estimates for potential projects.

If you are considering building a new house, an architect can be immensely helpful to you in the evaluation of prospective building sites. The Internet and real estate sections of newspapers abound with listings offering ready-to-build and even customizable plans. Typically, these one-size-fits-all plans presume a building site of universal sameness: flat and with no consideration whatsoever of the position of the house relative to the path of the sun, prevailing winds, or other natural or built features of the surrounding area.

Informed of your individual requirements and budget, an architect can evaluate

potential sites—rural, suburban, or urban—with an eye toward the natural and built environments. An architect is also specially attuned to the potentially restrictive requirements of the various municipalities and private subdivisions with respect to building lot setbacks and design criteria.

Compliance with Applicable Codes and Regulations

State boards of registration, as well as the standard agreement forms for architectural services, require an architect to review the laws, codes, and regulations that may be applicable to a project. As a skilled professional, an architect will craft the design to comply with requirements imposed by governmental authorities that have jurisdiction over the project. Building codes are now almost

This ubiquitous row house facade conceals the rich and expansive remodeling within.

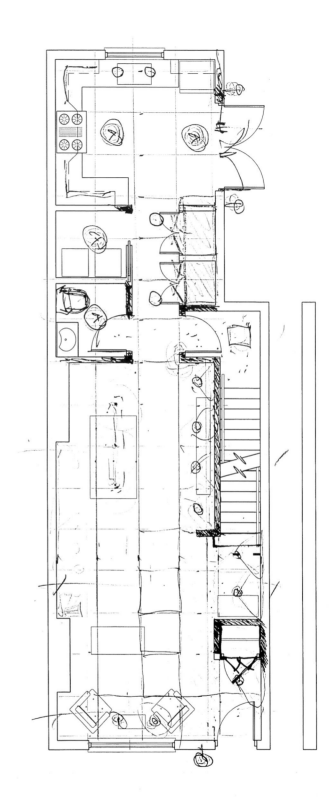

Plan of the first floor of the row house with author's notations for minor design refinements and light fixture locations.

Patio doors from the kitchen enframe a side courtyard featuring a tiled mosaic mural designed by a friend of the client's.

universal in the United States. However, zoning regulations are more particular to individual locales; they regulate a building's size and its relationship to the site.

Architects also have a working knowledge of how to design a home for access by persons with disabilities. Planning now for the future, your architect can accommodate the maneuverability needs of visiting parents and ensure the potential for your family to grow old in the secure and familiar environment of your home.

Preparation of Drawings and Specifications

The largest portion of an architect's professional services, and an architect's greatest skill,

is the development of the initial design idea into something that can be constructed. An architect is skilled at communicating the details of the required construction through drawings and specifications to the contractor. A complete set of drawings and specifications carefully document and describe in detail all the decisions you have made with your architect about the construction and detailing of the project—from the roof shingles to the kitchen sink.

Toward this end, architects keep abreast of the most current construction materials and building technologies. Most states require registered architects to complete a prescribed number of hours of continuing education each

Henry Hobson Richardson

Henry Hobson Richardson is regarded as one of America's most important architects—a giant of a man in talent, size, and personality. The series of houses Richardson designed toward the end of his career represent architectural achievement of the highest order. Among them is the Glessner House on Prairie Avenue in Chicago.

In 1885, John J. Glessner, vice president of an agricultural machinery manufacturer that later merged into International Harvester, hired Richardson to design his house on Millionaire's Row, which included the residences of the Armour, Field, Kimball, and Pullman families. In his memoir, Glessner called Richardson the "most dominating" person he had ever seen and one who was "inclined to be lawless about social conventions."[2] Glessner's impression, no doubt, was reinforced by Richardson's fondness of presenting photos of himself dressed as a monk to his clients!

Completed in 1887, the Glessner House is splendidly preserved, open to the public, and one of the major monuments of American domestic architecture.

[2] James F. O'Gorman, *Living Architecture: A Biography of H. H. Richardson* (New York: Simon & Schuster, 1977).

year. The American Institute of Architects requires its members to complete eighteen continuing-education hours per year. AIA course topics include health, safety, and welfare; codes, regulations, and standards; sustainability and green building; construction management; natural hazards; building science; and more.

An architect can save you time and money by recommending materials and systems that fit uniquely within the requirements and budget of your individual project. Even the conceptually simple project of a kitchen remodeling can reduce the most stalwart shopper to tears when he or she is confronted with the multitude of options for faucets alone. I am careful to judge my client's capacity to evaluate multiple choices, and then I craft a presentation of a limited number of selections that are both appropriate to the overall design context and within the budget of the project.

Coordination of Other Design Professionals

At Taliesin, we were inculcated to undertake all of the design responsibilities inherent in a project, including the detailing and selection of the interior finishes and furnishings. Frank Lloyd Wright notoriously designed even the kitchen china for some projects. Many architects don't take their design responsibilities to this extent. However, to ensure that everything goes smoothly, an architect coordinates the work of

Built-in furnishings and a discreet palette of materials compose an artful and expressive interior environment.

any specialty consultants that a project may require. Depending on the scope of the project, an architect might oversee the services of professional engineers for structural, electrical, and mechanical systems (heating, plumbing, air-conditioning); civil engineers for complex site work; landscape architects and horticulturalists for landscape design; and interior designers or decorators.

Selection of a Contractor

An architect can help you to identify and select a contractor whose skills and experience are best suited to your project. Many architects will provide you with a list of builders with whom they have worked successfully on projects similar to yours. Your architect can help you determine whether to solicit competitive bids from multiple contractors or negotiate a proposal with an individual contractor. The difference between competitive bids and negotiated proposals is explained in greater detail in chapter 4.

Administration of the Contract with the Contractor

The intrinsic value of a well-prepared set of drawings and specifications is revealed during the construction of the project when an architect, acting as your representative, administers the contract for construction between you and the contractor. The architect oversees the construction process to ensure that all requirements are fulfilled. Here is a sample of how this role of your architect is written in a client's contract:

The Architect, as a representative of the Owner, shall visit the site at intervals appropriate to the stage of the Contractor's operations, or as otherwise agreed by the Owner and the Architect in Article 2.8, (1) to become generally familiar with and to keep the Owner informed about the progress and quality of the portion of the Work completed, (2) to endeavor to guard the Owner against defects and deficiencies in the Work, and (3) to determine in general if the Work is being performed in a manner indicating

Collectively, this row house is greater than the sum of its parts.

LIVING ROOM/DINING COVE FOR TONI AULT

A partially rendered elevation drawing of the row house used to convey to the client the visual qualities of the finished space.

The Value of an Architect

A discreet extension of the dormer on this early-twentieth-century Tudor Revival house affords the opportunity for a generous master bathroom within.

SIDE ELEVATION ¼"=1'-0"
ALTERATIONS TO THE MARCUS RESIDENCE
GERALD LEE MOROSCO, ARCHITECT
06-25-91

Exterior elevation drawing of the Tudor Revival house.

that the Work, when fully completed, will be in accordance with the Contract Documents.

Adapted with permission from AIA Document B151-1977. © 1997 American Institute of Architects.

The architect is the singular skilled design professional who has the essential comb-ination of education, training, experience, and artistic vision to help you construct or remodel your home. As planner, designer, mediator, coordinator, business administrator, and counselor, an architect contributes real and lasting value through the entire process of designing and constructing or remodeling your home.

Although most architects have the skills to contribute such value, you will realize the best outcome for your investment by finding the architect with whom you can best cultivate an open and communicative relationship.

How to Find an Architect

At the conclusion of my presentations on how to work with an architect at various forums across the country, the most frequently asked question I receive from homeowners is, "How do I find an architect?"

Based on the answers from people in the audi-ences and by way of experience in my own practice, the most common and the best method for seeking an architect is to ask for recommendations from friends, coworkers, and acquaintances who have had previous experience in working with an architect. Not

The Value of an Architect

unlike seeking referrals for an accountant, lawyer, or dentist, word of mouth remains one of the most reliable means of introduction. Keep in mind, however, that one client's Prince Charming may well turn out to be another's toad, and no amount of kissing will achieve the transformation if the essential chemistry between the parties is just not right.

In most areas of the country, there are a great number of architects and architectural firms you might consider as potential partners for the conception and delivery of a residential project. Nevertheless, with a little investigation, you will quickly discern that many architects and architectural firms simply do not engage in residential practice at all. Of those that may consider such work, fewer still will entertain projects for alterations or additions to existing dwellings. Others may be quite particular about their comfort or capability of working in specific architectural styles.

The standard Yellow Pages remains a dependable resource. It lists just about every practicing architect in any given locale. Identifying a potential architect in this way may require some effort, as most professionals with small residential practices can afford only a basic listing that sheds little light on their suitability for your project.

If your project calls for something particular in terms of a style (e.g., Arts and Crafts) or has other special requirements (your house is in a

historic district, must be designed with hypoallergenic materials, or requires cutting-edge energy systems), you may have to expand your search beyond your immediate geographical area to find an architect best suited to your project. There are, of course, additional considerations for projects undertaken at a distance.

Many chapters of the American Institute of Architects offer directories of member architects and firms with detailed descriptions of their practices. A number of chapters (such as those in Boston, Massachusetts; Asheville, North Carolina; and Pittsburgh, Pennsylvania) offer high-quality printed directories and Web sites that list the services offered by their member architects. These directories should not be overlooked in your search for the appropriate architect.

The Web site of the Asheville, North Carolina, AIA chapter states that "over 90 percent of the architect-designed construction in the United States is handled by AIA members." I suspect that a significant amount of the work on single-family homes lies within that excluded 10 percent since many small residential architects either practice in areas in which there is not strong chapter representation or simply cannot afford the membership dues.

Beyond the resources that are exclusive to members of the AIA, the Internet in general

A meticulously detailed fireplace offers an inviting seating area in the remodeled Tudor Revival master bedroom suite.

offers a panoply of options for searching out and identifying architects. Many sites, however, remain but simple recitations of the information available in the Yellow Pages. Some require architects to pay to be listed or require that they complete detailed questionnaires that many, particularly small, practitioners don't have the time to fill out.

After identifying one or more architects suitable for your project, you should interview your candidates, just as you would interview a doctor, lawyer, or other professional whose services you require. You, the prospective client, should pose essential questions about your project in an initial conversation over the telephone.

Precious floor space in the Tudor Revival is maximized with built-in dressers and cabinets and a window seat that conceals the existing radiator in the master bedroom.

Renovation Information Network

The Renovation Information Network (RIN) is a program developed by the nonprofit Community Design Center of Pittsburgh, Pennsylvania. The program pairs interested homeowners with architects for a one-time, low-cost consultation. RIN has emerged as a model for providing homeowners access to affordable introductory architectural services. RIN has been successful in Pittsburgh since 1996 and has sparked interest in other cities, such as Hartford, Atlanta, Detroit, and Philadelphia.

RIN's goals are:

• Expand homeowners' awareness of renovation options.
• Encourage positive interior and exterior improvements that add value, not only to the individual home but to the community as a whole.
• Foster energy-saving improvements and strategies that conserve homeowners' resources for other uses, including reinvestment in their homes.

An independent audit of the pilot program discovered that nearly 90 percent of users found the program helpful or very helpful, and more than half of the participants indicated the volunteer architect contributed significantly to their renovation plans. Almost all, 97 percent, would recommend the RIN program to a friend.

To determine if a similar resource is available in your area, contact your local AIA chapter, community design center, preservation organization, or other group committed to the quality of the built environment in your community.

The American Institute of Architects

Many architects are members of the American Institute of Architects (AIA). The AIA is a national professional association that promotes and supports the practice of architecture. With headquarters in Washington, DC, and with more than three hundred state and local chapters, the AIA has been a committed advocate of excellence in the built environment and service to the larger community since its inception in 1857.

The 75,000 AIA member architects are required to comply with the AIA Code of Ethics, which dictates guidelines for the highest standards of professionalism, integrity, and competence. The code addresses architects' responsibilities to the public, which the profession serves and enriches; to the clients and users of architecture, who help shape the built environment; and to the art and science of architecture, the body of knowledge and creativity that supports the profession.

Adapted with permission from the American Institute of Architects, 1735 New York Ave., NW, Washington, DC, 20006.

The conveniences of a contemporary bath are realized by use of traditional materials consistent with the style of the original Tudor Revival house.

Your Initial Meeting with an Architect

You should insist on meeting with the architect who will actually work with you on your project. This first meeting might take place at the architect's office, at your home or office, or at some other location. I frequently invite prospective clients to meet with me at my own home. There is nothing better than an opportunity to experience an architect's work firsthand. While many architects do not charge for an initial interview, some do, and you should ask if there is a fee during your first conversation with the architect over the phone.

A face-to-face interview is critical because it offers you and the architect an opportunity to test the potential chemistry between you. Depending on the size of your project, you may be working closely with your architect for many months, and your relationship may extend to future projects as well. It is important, if you are undertaking your project as a couple, that you and your significant other attend interviews with prospective architects.

Allow at least an hour for the initial interview. If you are unfamiliar with the architect's work, he or she should show you examples of past projects. I typically furnish a potential client with at least three references for past projects similar in scope and scale to the prospective project. I ask that the individual visit the projects and speak with the homeowners. Most clients enjoy talking about their home-building experiences and will be forthcoming about their relationship with their architect—more so if the architect is not present. Builders can also serve as very good references. If you want to be thorough, speak with the builders of the houses of the architect's client references.

Remember, this first meeting is an opportunity for you to ask questions. Ask for clarification if there is something you do not understand. If the architect does not take the time to explain things in a way that you can understand, you may not have found your architect. You want an architect who listens and responds to your questions and with whom you feel comfortable.

An Investment of a Lifetime

For most people, the construction or remodeling of a home represents one of the largest financial investments of a lifetime. You should invest at least the amount of time and care you would to select a financial or legal advisor. To ensure a relationship built upon trust and confidence, you should choose the architect you feel can best provide professional services and creative artisanship to help you realize a home that satisfies your practical needs and fulfills your dreams.

Accomplished within the Tudor Revival's expanded dormer, a shallow closet becomes a dressing boudoir.

Twenty Questions for Interviewing an Architect

1. Do you have a specific design style? Can you show me examples of your past design work?

2. What distinguishes you from other architects?

3. Can you provide a list of past clients with whom you have worked?

4. How busy are you? How many other projects are you working on?

5. Will I be dealing directly with you or someone else in your firm? Who will be designing my project?

6. How interested are you in my project?

7. How will you gather information about my needs and goals?

8. What do you expect me to provide in order for you to begin work on my project?

9. What do you see as my project's important issues or considerations? What are its challenges?

10. How will you establish priorities and make decisions about my project?

11. How do you organize the design process?

12. What are the steps in the design process?

13. What will you show me along the way to explain the project? Will I see models, drawings, or sketches?

14. How long do you anticipate it will take you to complete your portion of the project?

15. How do you establish fees? When will you expect payment?

16. What do you anticipate your fee will be for this project?

17. What is your experience and track record with cost estimating?

18. If the scope of the project changes later, will there be additional fees? How will those fees be justified?

19. If the contractors' bids exceed my budget, will you revise the design? Is there an additional fee for such redesign?

20. What services do you provide during construction?

Adapted with permission of www.architects.org. Material was first published by the Boston Society of Architects.

Beeswax, turpentine, boiled linseed oil, and yellow ochre pigment were the ingredients of the stain finish used on plaster surfaces throughout the author's home.

DECIDING WHERE TO
Build or Buy

The American Dream

The acquisition of land conjures up an image that is essentially American. What came to be described, upon its discovery in the fifteenth century, as the New World continues to provide opportunities for us today to pursue the American Dream of buying a plot of land and constructing a house.

Much of the land in the United States, however, is currently being exploited today through residential construction. Cranberry Township, north of Pittsburgh, Pennsylvania, has been held out nationally as an example of what many consider to be ecologically questionable development. The rapacious rate at which arable farmland there has been supplanted with ubiquitous housing developments and strip malls is distressing. At an even faster pace, pristine desert land in the arid Southwest, once considered uninhabitable, is being developed through the expanding

The author's home before and after a little love and a lot of design help.

distribution of diminishing water resources to support the growth of entire new communities.

A contrasting development model is more sustainable and ecologically sound. In a number of urban areas, former industrial lands and disinvested neighborhoods are being reclaimed and redeveloped with new housing. Foremost in thinking of this kind is the Urban Land Institute, whose mission is to provide responsible leadership in the use of land to enhance the total environment. The institute promotes development that is environmentally sensitive, economically viable, community oriented, and sustainable.

Although every area must define what Smart Growth means at the local and regional levels, most proponents agree on some common characteristics.

- Development is economically viable and preserves open space and natural resources.
- Land-use planning is comprehensive, integrated, and regional.
- Public, private, and nonprofit sectors collaborate on smart growth and development issues to achieve mutually beneficial outcomes.
- Certainty and predictability are inherent to the development process.
- Infrastructure is maintained and enhanced to serve existing and new residents.
- Redevelopment of infill housing, brownfield sites, and obsolete buildings is actively pursued.
- Urban centers and neighborhoods are integral components of a healthy regional economy.
- Compact suburban development is integrated into existing commercial areas, new town centers, and/or near existing or planned transportation facilities.

- Development on the urban fringe integrates a mix of land uses, preserves open space, is fiscally responsible, and provides transportation options.

Deciding Where to Build with Your Architect

In the previous chapter, I discussed how an architect is helpful in the evaluation and selection of building sites. It is common to think of an architect when you are actually prepared to build, but few people recognize the value an architect can bring to the consideration of *where* to build. Prospective clients who have recently purchased land frequently contact me. They are excited and ready to begin work on the design of their new house. Unfortunately, in a number of instances, the land they've acquired proves to be less than ideal or, worse, actually unbuildable for reasons that are not readily apparent to them.

Most commonly, people identify the locale in which they prefer to live for personal reasons, such as a good school district, proximity to work, and so on. Once the general location is established, many people fall in love with a given piece of land based on its characteristics, especially its defining natural features. They fail to take into consideration a multitude of problems that may, quite literally, lie just beneath the surface, like subsurface groundwater or unstable soil that cannot support a foundation.

Pennsylvania Farmhouse

A well-to-do couple engaged me to consider their project to remodel an existing farmhouse and design a new comfortably removed guest cottage. They owned several hundred acres of picturesque rolling farm and forested land. I listened carefully to their detailed requirements for the project while we strolled about the land immediate to the existing farmhouse.

Prior to my engagement, they had made a substantial investment in developing the infrastructure of the area around the existing house and several outbuildings, landscaping, and paved access roads. It was immediately apparent to me, however, that despite their significant acreage, the existing house was located less than twenty feet from their property line!

Confronted with the possibility of the future development of that adjoining farmland, we quickly established that, rather than undertake a significant remodeling of the existing house, it would be more cost effective to construct an entirely new house in a more ideal location on their property and to simply make over the existing home as their guest cottage. For their new house, we identified a secluded site in the woods that was a comfortable distance from the property line but near enough to take advantage of their previous infrastructure improvements.

This vertical element at the head of the stair to the second floor of the author's home conceals mechanical ductwork as it forms a visual ascension to a skylight above.

There are also a number of human-imposed restrictions, including easements, right-of-ways, restrictive covenants, and zoning regulations, that may affect the suitability of a piece of land for building. An architect can help you identify these various factors, thereby giving you the opportunity to consider their potential influence on your building program and budget.

Wherever you might choose to build, there are essentially two types of available land: unimproved, or raw, and improved, or buildable. Improved land that has been developed in preparation for building is frequently subdivided into smaller parcels that are sold as lots. Land characterized as improved implies that connections to utility services are present. An architect can help you investigate the availability of the connections to utilities, as well as other special requirements that might obligate you to install other improvements, such as sidewalks, landscaping, or even street lighting. I encourage anyone undertakng a search for land on which to build to consult with an architect before committing to purchase.

Zoning and Other Governmental Regulations

Nearly every piece of land falls under the jurisdiction of a city or county that regulates its development and use by way of zoning regulations. You may recall seeing roadside signs,

Fallingwater

Fallingwater, Frank Lloyd Wright's magnum opus designed for Pittsburgh department store magnate Edgar Kaufmann and his family, is perhaps the most recognized single-family house in the world.

Almost two decades after its conception, in a television interview with Hugh Downs, Wright described the placement of the house: "There in a beautiful forest was a solid high rock ledge rising beside a waterfall, and the natural thing seemed to be to cantilever the house from that rock bank over the falling water."[1] When Wright first presented the concept to the client, Kaufmann responded, "I thought you would place the house near the waterfall, not over it." Wright said quietly, "E. J., I want you to live with the waterfall, not just to look at it, but for it to become an integral part of your lives."[2] The story of Wright's placement of the house on that site reveals, in the extreme, the value that an architect can bring to the process of evaluating a building site.

[1] Wright, Frank Lloyd, interview by Hugh Downs, National Broadcasting Company, at Taliesin, 1953.

[2] Byron Keeler Mosher, letter, January 20, 1974.

common at the borders of many municipalities, that state, "Welcome to Anytown, USA. . . . Zoned for your protection."

Zoning regulations establish the permitted uses of buildings. They also define allowable height and area for buildings, as well as the setbacks from property lines. Generally regulations provide "protection" by restricting the juxtaposition of structures with incompatible uses, such as the placement of a meat-packing plant in a residential neighborhood. An architect will become familiar with all of the regulations applicable to your property as one of the initial steps in a project.

If your potential site is on newly subdivided farmland, it is important to determine the zoning for your lot as well as for the adjacent parcels. It would be unfortunate to buy a five-acre parcel only to discover that the adjoining property is being zoned for half-acre sites, leaving you amidst a sea of other houses. Conversely, many homeowners on redeveloped rural parcels have been distressed to discover, upon hearing the predawn whirl of agricultural machinery, that their newly constructed dream home is adjacent to a working farm.

A young couple took me to visit their building site on a hilltop with stunning views of the rolling countryside in all directions. As they enthusiastically paced out the location they planned for their dream home, the shadow of

a low-flying jet swept across the "living room" with an accompanying roar. In their many previous visits, they had failed to realize that the site was directly under the final approach path to a major airport.

In such rural areas, but also within urban areas undergoing redevelopment, the local government can modify or change the zoning regulations to adapt to changing needs of the community. You and your architect can obtain copies of development and land use plans, as well as notices of any proposed zoning changes, at the planning or building departments of most communities. Whether your land is rural or urban, it would be beneficial to get some sense of what might happen to the area within the next ten or twenty years. You may not be pleased to discover plans for a road expansion or development of a shopping mall after the completion of your new home.

In addition to basic zoning regulations, some locations have overlay zoning, special districts, or other ordinances that prescribe additional restrictions on how you can develop and build on a property. These are commonly found on properties where construction may have an adverse impact on environmental features and resources, such as hillsides and watersheds, or on natural vegetation or wildlife. Some restrictions protect scenic views or guarantee public access to

In the kitchen of the author's home,
note the cork flooring and maple cabinetry,
which also continue throughout the house.

recreation areas, such as beaches or water-fronts. Others regulate the appearance of built structures in designated historic districts or natural landscapes.

Deed Restrictions and Other Limitations

Many properties have restrictive covenants and other conditions that are recorded on the deed. These have nothing to do with zoning or other governmental regulations but could significantly affect the use of your property.

An easement is the legal right to use another's land for a specified purpose. Easements can be granted for the building or maintaining of roads, sewage lines, electrical lines, or other public or private utilities. An example is an easement affording a utility company the right to bury a gas-transmission pipeline through a property. Right-of-way is a specific type of easement that affords the legal right to pass along a specific route through property belonging to another. A common right-of-way

Deciding Where to Build or Buy

deed is granted to a governing body for the widening, construction, or maintaining of a public road.

Restrictive covenants are another type of deed restriction that typically apply to a group of homes or lots within developments or subdivisions. Such covenants attempt to protect property values by regulating the appearance of homes and restricting the kinds of activities that can take place. Commonly referred to as CC&Rs (Covenants, Codes, and Restrictions) they normally do the following:

• Stipulate the minimum size for a residence.
• Establish the type of construction.
• Define building setbacks and easements.
• Set rules for fencing, landscaping, and accessory structures.

Other common restrictions that could affect the design and construction of your house include specific lists of permitted and prohibited building materials and design guidelines that establish allowable styles. It is also not uncommon for such regulations to put forth a list of preselected contractors from which you must select the builder for your house.

Your architect can help determine the effect various restrictions may have on your building plans—from practical considerations (Will the building setback requirements restrict the size of your home?) to more thoughtful observations

Built-in cabinets define the dressing room space adjacent to the master bedroom in the author's home.

(Might a utility easement portend an unsightly string of power lines across your property in the future?). Many architects have knowledge of and experience with zoning ordinances and regulations and, if necessary, can work together with your legal counsel to prepare a case for variances or other exceptions that may be required for a project.

Undeveloped Land

Unless you intend to live "off the grid," utilizing solar or wind power, the costs associated with establishing utility connections can be significant. You and your architect will consider the expense within the context of your total project budget. You will also need to verify the availability and locations for water, sewer, electricity, gas, and telecommunications. The need to drill a well or install a septic system can add significant cost to the project. Keep in mind that before you can calculate these expenses, you will need to determine if there is water available to be drilled for and whether the soil can support a septic system in accordance with applicable health department regulations. Also be sure to secure estimates for extending the required services to your proposed building site.

Soil, Topography, and Other Site Conditions

Depending on the region, your architect may ask you to undertake soil testing to determine the suitability of the undeveloped land for construction. Certain soil conditions, such as expansive clays or subsurface rock formations, can render a perfectly beautiful site useless or add tens of thousands of dollars in cost that will, quite literally, get poured into the ground.

Conditions above ground can affect the cost and feasibility of a project as well. Contractors will increase their prices in relation to the actual (or perceived) difficulty of getting to and from the project site. The space constraints of many urban projects can add cost

because there is inadequate space to park construction vehicles and to store materials.

I once evaluated a client's building site that was located just below the tree line in the mountains near Telluride, Colorado. The high altitude combined with the spectacular view literally took my breath away. The site was accessible only by snow tractor during the winter months, and the alpine weather conditions limited the time available for construction to essentially four months of the year. Even in clear weather, access to the site was via a long, slow, and bone-jarring jeep trail, which necessitated that most of the construction materials be flown in by helicopter. There were, in fact, builders in the region who specialized in working under such conditions. However, the premium on the construction nearly quadrupled the cost of a like structure in the town itself.

Conditions for building at a site high in the mountains can indeed be as challenging as those found at the seashore. But, between such extremes, every site presents a particular set of climatic conditions that an architect is especially attuned to consider when designing your house.

Site Hunting with Your Architect

Vacant land is not the only option for a building site for your new house. In older neighborhoods across America, ranch houses, bungalows, and other examples of the more

This view from the master bedroom of the author's home portrays the spacious nature of the interior design.

modest dream homes of bygone eras are being replaced with new larger homes that are more in sync with the rising value of the land beneath them. The *tear-down* has become an almost ubiquitous term in the advertising lexicon of today's real estate agent. While this radical practice speaks volumes about the consumption-based culture in which we live, there is much to be said for building or remodeling a home in an established neighborhood.

The utility infrastructure is typically in place in established neighborhoods. Although the electricity, water, and sewer connections may need to be upgraded or the capacities increased, the savings over establishing new services on unimproved land can add significant savings to an overall project budget. An assessment of the existing house's conditions can offer insights to your architect regarding issues with drainage and soil conditions; for instance, dampness in the basement or cracks in the foundation walls can signal unstable soil conditions. There are also less tangible, but nonetheless valuable, benefits of preexisting services and amenities that an established neighborhood can offer. Consider the value of a mature landscape, for example.

House Hunting with Your Architect

Many land considerations—such as zoning, deed restrictions and conditions, and availability of utilities—are necessary to bear in mind before buying an existing house. Whereas the design of a home on a fresh parcel of land is limited only by the conditions of that particular site and your requirements, the potential of an existing house is more tightly constrained by factors like the construction quality, current conditions, architectural style, and the likelihood of recovering your investment.

Architects, as a part of their very nature, are space planners, and that nature is cultivated by their educations. The value of utilizing an architect to evaluate the potential of existing houses is much more apparent as the reference points are established. Regardless of your conceptual abilities, you can get a pretty good understanding of what a given space may become when your architect clearly describes how the space could be modified to meet your needs.

Many lenders and some states now require a certified home inspection before you can finalize the purchase of an existing single-family home. An entire industry has grown up to meet this requirement. Home inspectors, for the most part, have not been trained as architects, nor do many have any practical experience in construction. The best can identify the presence of serious mechanical and structural flaws in a house that can be translated into cost savings at the bargaining table. Your architect, however, can offer insight into the feasibility and costs of a myriad of repairs, alterations, and additions to any given house.

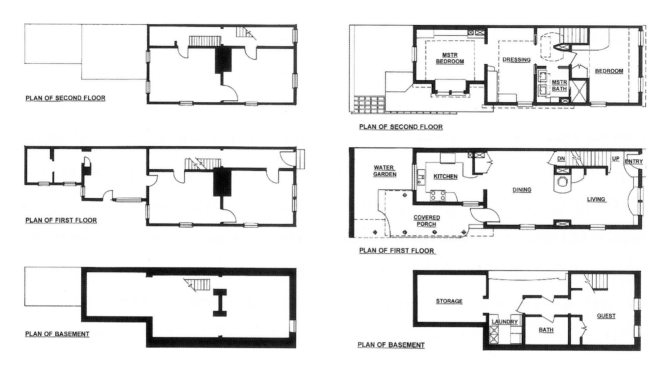

PLAN OF SECOND FLOOR

PLAN OF FIRST FLOOR

PLAN OF BASEMENT

PLAN OF SECOND FLOOR

MSTR BEDROOM   DRESSING   BEDROOM   MSTR BATH

PLAN OF FIRST FLOOR

WATER GARDEN   KITCHEN   DINING   LIVING   DN   UP   ENTRY   COVERED PORCH

PLAN OF BASEMENT

STORAGE   LAUNDRY   BATH   GUEST

These before and after floor plans of the author's home illustrate the careful articulation of the spaces within the narrow 16–foot-wide footprint.

I have cultivated a specialty niche working with real estate professionals. After clients narrow down their options to three or four houses with the help of their real estate agent, I walk through the first house with the prospective buyers. This typically reveals much about their lifestyle, preferences, and budget. Subsequent visits to their other choices further illuminate their wants and needs. I then produce a fairly quick evaluation of the most cost-effective choice for their renovation dollars.

In instances where the potential investment in the property and the projected improvements are substantial, I also produce a design concept from which we can actually prepare an estimate of probable cost for the work. Cost is sometimes not the primary consideration, in which case I help clients sort out their various impressions and true preferences.

Remodel, Add On, Move, or Rearrange the Furniture

I once provided an RIN consultation (see page 25) for a young couple with two children who lived in a small American foursquare-style house. They wanted to expand their home to accommodate their growing family. They carefully walked me through their concept of how they might add on to the house. They were clear about where they wanted the additional space they required but uncertain as to how to utilize the remaining space that "just didn't work out." It was quickly apparent to me that they did not, in fact, require additional space, but rather a more careful arrangement of their existing spaces. I was able to provide them with some quick drawings to guide them through the simple modifications with a contractor.

An artful juxtaposition of a medicine cabinet suspended on a mirrored wall beneath a skylight in the author's home.

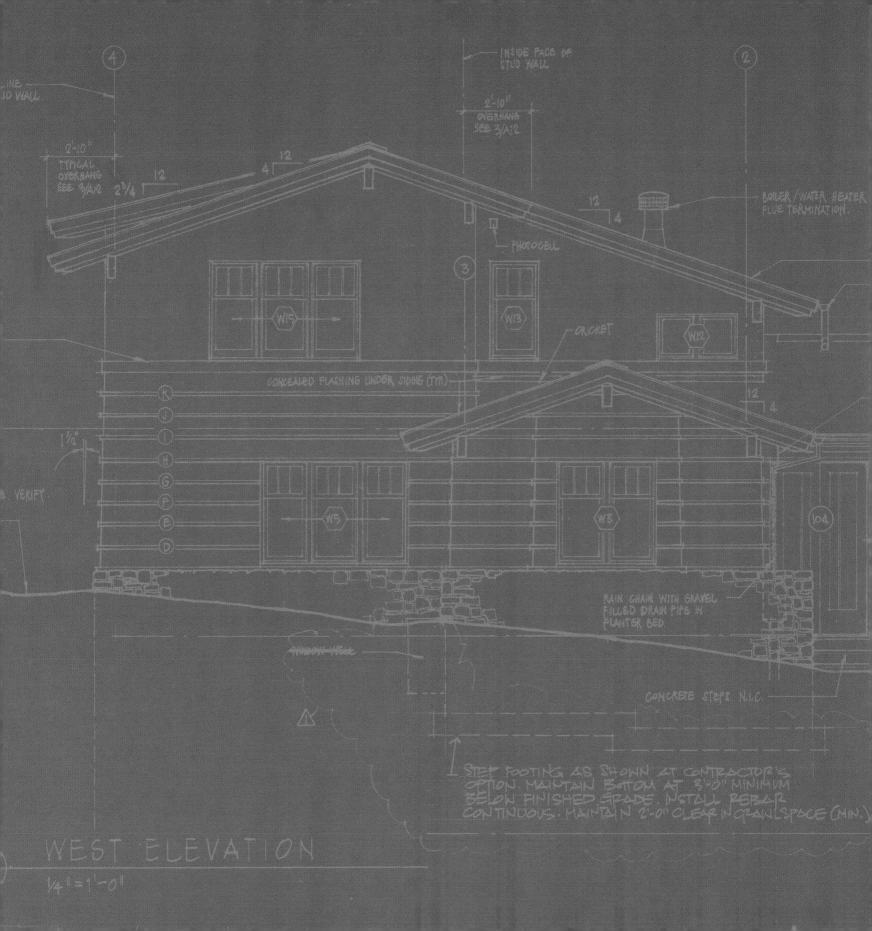

WEST ELEVATION

1/4" = 1'-0"

Part II

HOW DO YOU WORK WITH AN

Architect?

A color pencil interior perspective rendering presented to the client during the Schematic Design Phase.

THE AGREEMENT AND THE
Architect's Fee

Communicate Your Objectives

Now that you are getting down to business, it is important to establish a complete understanding of your objectives and constraints with your architect. The points below can help to solidify your goals, budget, and schedule. You have communicated much of this information previously during your initial discussions with your architect, but reviewing it will be valuable as you begin to work through the terms of your contract with your architect.

- Describe your current living circumstance (house, condominium, or apartment)
  - What do you like about it?
  - What don't you like?
  - What's missing?
- Why do you want to build a house or add to or renovate your current home?
  - Do you need more room?
  - Do you want to scale down because your children are grown and moving on?

HOUSE ON STRAWBERRY HILL FOR MR. & MRS. CHARLES G. WALTON
CLARION, PENNSYLVANIA
GERALD LEE MOROSCO ARCHITECT

- What is your lifestyle?
  - Are you at home a great deal?
  - How much time do you spend in the living areas of your house— bedrooms, kitchen, den, or office?
  - Do you work at home?
  - Do you entertain often?
  - Is your lifestyle changing?
- How much can you realistically afford to invest in this project?
- How soon would you like your new house or addition to be completed? Are there any time constraints or impending significant events—wedding, bar mitzvah, childbirth— that might impact the project?
- How much time and energy are you willing to invest to maintain your home?

- If you are thinking of constructing an addition to your house, what functions/activities will be housed in the new space?
- What kinds of spaces do you need—bedrooms, expanded kitchen, bathrooms, and so on?
- What do you think the addition/renovation/new house should look like?
- If planning a new house, what do you envision in this new house that you do not presently enjoy?
- If you are contemplating building a new house from the ground up, do you have a site selected?
- Do you have strong ideas about design styles? What are your design preferences?
- Which family member will be the primary contact with the architect, contractor, and

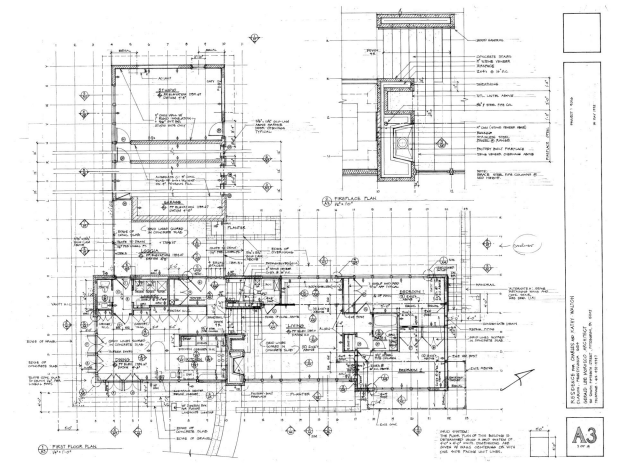

Detailed construction drawing floor plan for the contemporary split-level house on the facing page, which is shown in a color pencil Schematic Design perspective.

others involved in designing and building the project?

• How much time do you have to be involved in the design and construction process?

• Do you plan to execute or direct any of the actual construction work yourself?

• How much disruption in your life can you tolerate to add on to or renovate your house?

Adapted with permission from www.architects.org. Material first published by the Boston Society of Architects.

Careful planning and discussions about the scope of the project, compensation, and scheduling with your architect at the outset will help establish open communication and ensure a successful relationship.

Drafting a Contract with Your Architect

Having found an architect for your project, all parties will be excited and eager to craft a design solution. At this juncture it is important to take time to draft a thorough written agreement that outlines the roles and responsibilities of each party. The contract should detail the fees, schedules, and tasks so that you can monitor the project's progress every step of the way.

A written agreement serves to guard against unintended or unwanted results as well as

The Agreement and the Architect's Fee

establish goals and expectations for the relationship. In the absence of a written agreement, there could be misunderstandings between you and your architect that may be both expensive and time-consuming to resolve.

The misunderstanding between architect Mies van der Rohe and his client discussed on page 73 provides an extreme example of the degree of misunderstanding that can develop. The importance of a written contract cannot be overstated.

Since 1996, California state law has required that any architect who agrees to provide architectural services to a client draw up a written contract. Although the statutory provision allows clients to state in writing that services can be started before the contract is executed or that they do not want a written contract, a written agreement is strongly recommended.

Many architects utilize standard forms of agreement prepared by the American Institute of Architects (AIA). The AIA's Standard Form of Agreement between Owner and Architect has been continually refined and updated since it was first copyrighted in 1917. As that standard agreement has evolved to address contingencies in projects of varying scope and scale, it has become increasingly ponderous and in parts difficult to understand, even for many architects. For this reason, many residential architects utilize an abbreviated form of the

standard AIA agreement or craft their own agreement built upon that boilerplate.

Take time to review the agreement carefully. Certainly you have the right to question and change the terms of the contract before signing it. Ask as many questions as necessary until you get the answers you need in language you can understand. You may also want to have your legal counsel review the agreement before you sign it. The true value of any agreement remains essentially dependent on the good will of the parties. At its best, an agreement serves to establish a written record of a mutual and specific understanding between a client and the architect. You and your architect should each retain original signature copies of the agreement.

Important Items to Include in a Contract
The California Architects Board again affords a good example of what to include in an agreement with your architect. The state requires that a written contract for architectural services contain, at a minimum, the following crucial items.

- Name and address of the architect.
- Name and address of the client.
- The business form of the architect's practice (i.e., corporation, sole proprietorship, or limited liability partnership).
- Description of the professional services to be provided by the architect to the client.

- Description of compensation applicable to the contract and method of payment agreed upon by both parties.
- Description of the procedure the architect and client will use to accommodate additional services. (Some examples are discussed later in this chapter under the heading Additional Costs, page 58.)
- Description of the procedure to be used by either party to terminate the contract.

Your agreement for architectural services should clearly and completely define the goals and expectations of both parties for the project. In addition to the above items, a thorough agreement could also include the following.

- The location and address of the project.
- Description of the project, including any special requirements.
- Description of the architect's basic services and proposed fee for these services.
- Estimated construction budget and an itemization of what it includes.
- Contingencies for escalation of architect fee and construction budget resulting from changes in the project scope during design and construction phase, or an outline of when the client's approval must be given in order for the architect to proceed to the next phase.
- Definition of reimbursable expenses and the procedures for authorization and compensation.

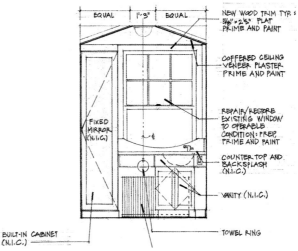

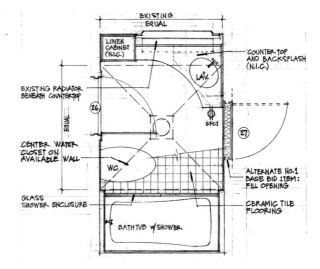

Bathroom vanity with construction drawing floor plan and elevation.

The Agreement and the Architect's Fee

Cautions for Couples

If you are undertaking a project as a couple, it is especially important that you both understand the process of working with an architect and that you both participate in the process throughout. If only one of you will be making the decisions, you should clearly articulate this to your architect at the outset. Online architect chat rooms and articles in professional architect journals abound with horror stories of residential projects gone awry after the silent or absent spouse appeared late in the process to express dissatisfaction with the design or some project detail. After sensing a lack of agreement between spouses, not uncommon in residential work, I have at times somewhat jokingly made reference to my second vocation as a marriage counselor.

Some years ago I worked with a newlywed middle-aged couple. Both the woman and man had had previous homes and families, and they came to the process with a well-established set of likes and dislikes for the new house they would share. We were planning the remodel of their master bedroom and bathroom suite. During the process of defining their requirements, I inquired if it was important for them to have a discreet toilet compartment, as is typical today in many large master bathrooms. In a simultaneous response to my question, she blurted out, "Absolutely," as he declared, "Not an issue." The final design incorporated a separate toilet compartment.

- Listing of project consultants who may be needed and a definition of the procedures for hiring and compensating them.
- Required retainer fee and how and when it will be applied to the total fee for services.
- Schedule of when architect fee payments are due and in what amounts.
- Statement of whether the architect provides assistance with bidding and/or establishing a contract between a contractor and the client and if it is part of the basic services or an additional service.
- Statement of whether the architect provides construction observation and if this is part of the basic services or is an additional service.
- Statement of who is responsible for keeping the project account records and when they can be reviewed.
- Statement of who owns the project documents.
- Procedure for handling disputes (e.g., arbitration or mediation, depending on state law) between the parties should the need arise.
- Instructions for how final payment will be computed if the agreement is terminated.

Drafting the Contract

Do not assume your architect will interpret everything you discuss with him or her in the same way you do. Remember, unless you make yourself clearly heard, your architect may not realize that you do not understand contract terms or descriptions of services that are very familiar to him or her. Many of the most common problems encountered in the

A contemporary working kitchen crafted out of the former butler's pantry, breakfast nook, and kitchen spaces in an early-twentieth-century house.

process of working with an architect can be traced back to misunderstandings or unreasonable expectations that could have been corrected with a thorough review of an agreement at the outset. Good communication, important to the success of any relationship, is essential to working with an architect.

It is the practice in my office to take notes of every meeting, thereby creating a written record of the verbal communications with our clients. These notes are issued as minutes and distributed (e-mail can be used) to all attendees to review and make corrections. These written records give everyone involved an opportunity to assure understanding of decisions. Throughout the course of the project, you should insist on having a written record, regardless of form, of important decisions.

The Architect's Fee

The issue of how architects are compensated for their services can be confusing. No two architects bill for work in exactly the same way. Federal antitrust laws effectively prohibit architects from collectively establishing a more or less uniform pricing structure like that familiar to the general public in the real estate industry. Accordingly, architectural fees are established in a variety of ways and can vary widely depending on the specific nature of a project and actual services that the architect provides.

Most simply, architects are compensated for the time they spend on a project, as are many other professional service providers, including accountants and attorneys. Like these other professionals, architects' billing rates vary widely, based on their level of experience and reputation, the size and location of their practice, and the specific task at hand. The size of architectural practices can range from one person working solo out of his or her house to large firms employing hundreds of people. A nascent practitioner in a small community may charge significantly less than $100 per hour, whereas, in a major metropolitan area, a seasoned professional with an established reputation may command many times that hourly rate.

Many established practitioners have developed their fee structures based on personal experience over time. While architects understand the structure and calculation of their compensation, it is often misunderstood by clients. You should ask your architect to carefully review the method of compensation as well as those portions of the agreement that describe conditions under which he or she may be afforded extra compensation for additional services. Be sure to hire a qualified architect, not the least expensive one.

For residential work, architectural fees are typically calculated based on one, or a combination of, the following methods:

Time-Based Fee

Many residential architects charge an hourly billing rate. In this arrangement, an architect's salary, benefits, overhead, and profit are included in an established rate schedule for designated personnel. A schedule of the billing rates for each person who might work on your project should be included in the contract.

Typically the rates for the principal architect and senior staff are noted next to their names, whereas rates for support staff are noted next to their titles. For example: "Principal's time at the fixed rate of One Hundred Fifty Dollars ($150.00) per hour. For the purposes of this Agreement, the Principals are: John Doe, AIA, and Sarah Smith, AIA. Technical Level II time at the fixed rate of Fifty-Five Dollars ($55.00) per hour. For the purposes of this Agreement, Technical Level II personnel include intern architects awaiting licensure and clerical staff."

In small firms, the same personnel may bill at different hourly rates, dependent upon the task on which they are working. For instance, one person may have a higher rate for time spent in meetings than for time spent on drafting tasks. Some highly compensated principals may have a lower billing rate for travel or other "noncreative" tasks. Again, these details should be clearly spelled out in your agreement.

Stipulated Sum or Fixed Fee

From a client's perspective, the stipulated sum approach is the most easily understood method of compensation since payment is stated as a fixed dollar amount. A variation is compensation on a time-based method with a not-to-exceed total or maximum fee. Any variation of this method requires a very clear description of the architect's services based upon a well-established understanding of the scope and scale of the project.

Percentage of Construction Cost or Cost of Work

A fee calculated by multiplying the overall construction cost by an agreed-upon percentage remains one of the most time-honored and traditional methods of compensation for architectural services. Although increasingly less common in commercial work, where the scope and scale of a project are more likely to be clearly established at the outset, this method continues to be employed by many residential architects.

The method is deceptively simple to calculate. Some complexity arises in establishing the definition of the construction cost or, as described in some agreements, "the cost of the work." You should take care to understand precisely how the construction cost will be determined and how the architect's fee will be calculated in the event that the project is abandoned before construction or if some portion of the design is not executed.

Standard AIA agreements define construction cost as "the total cost or, to the extent the Project is not completed, the estimated cost to the Owner of all elements of the Project designed or specified by the Architect." In a straightforward project where there is a single contract with a general contractor to construct the entire project designed by the architect, the amount of that contract will be the cost basis for calculating the architect's fee. But what if you intend to purchase and possibly even install some of the materials for the project yourself? Or perhaps you own a barn full of old lumber that you would like to incorporate into the project. Most agreements calculate the price of such labor or material as "the cost at current market rates of labor and materials furnished by the Owner."

Taken at face value, a fee based upon cost can result in misunderstanding when a value-conscious client seeks to save on the construction cost and architectural fees by contributing previously owned or discounted materials and/or his or her own labor. If you contemplate savings during construction by any means, you should discuss this with your architect during your initial meetings so that you can agree upon a fair, equitable, and mutually understandable method of compensation. Obviously, your architect will not reduce his or her scope of services in proportion to any savings you might achieve by furnishing materials or by contributing your own labor.

The Agreement and the Architect's Fee

Calculating the Fee Based on Percentage of Construction Cost

Many clients are troubled by a sneaking suspicion that their architect may be working to increase the cost of the project so as to increase his or her compensation. This is as unlikely as it is would be unethical. Rather than harbor this feeling, or any other concern, you should clear the air by means of a candid discussion with your architect.

Much of the cost in a custom residential project is in the finishes, fixtures, and equipment. What substantive difference could there be, you may wonder, in the time required for your architect to incorporate a $250 faucet versus a $2,500 faucet into the design of your powder room—or tile that costs $2 per square foot versus $200 per square foot into your kitchen? This is a fair and common question to which I can respond from direct experience: both the available choices, as well as the amount of time you will spend considering them with your architect, increase in relation to the cost of those items. This increase in time carries through the entire development of the project. You can be sure that care and attention to the specification, handling, and installation of a $2,500 faucet well exceeds that of one that costs only ten percent as much.

When an architect bases his or her fee on a percentage of project cost, there is invariably

The Client's Cost in Perspective

When you examine the architect's fee in relation to the total cost of the project, the value of employing an architect far outweighs the cost.

The following chart provides a theoretical breakdown of the total cost of a project employing an architect:

	Cost	% of Total Cost
Land Purchase Price	$100,000	11%
House Construction Cost	$200,000	22%
Architect's Fee @ 15% of Construction Cost	$30,000	3%
Miscellaneous Closing Fees	$10,000	1%
Landscaping and Driveway	$12,000	1%
Interest on $270,000 30-Year Mortgage @ 8%	$443,220	50%
Taxes @ $4,000 per annum for 25 years	$100,000	11%
TOTAL	$895,220	

A full-scale model of an unrealized 1953 apartment designed by Frank Lloyd Wright.

an underlying time-based calculation that supports the fee and this is based on prior experience. In my own practice, once a project has proceeded well into the development of the design, we are able to work the calculation for the percentage fee backwards by dividing the hourly cost of our time invested in the project by the completed percentage of our entire scope of services to arrive at an estimated construction cost for the project. In many projects, we can utilize this reverse calculation to check our preliminary cost estimates.

Many architects favor the percentage-fee method because it is relatively easy to calculate, and it avoids the sometimes uncomfortable task, inherent in time-based billings, of explaining in detail how time was spent on the project. Also, many residential projects tend to fluctuate in scope, scale, and cost during their development. The percentage-based fee allows

the architect's compensation to move up and down with the evolving project cost and avoids the potential necessity of renegotiating compensation.

You will find that most architects charge anywhere from 5 to 25 percent of the construction cost of a residential project, with fees in the middle range—from 10 percent to 20 percent— being most common. Percentage-based fees vary, as do hourly billing rates.

In considering the cost of architectural services, the well-worn adage "you get what you pay for" is all too true. While differences in the reputation, experience, size, and location of an architect's practice may account for some variation in fees, differences in the actual services provided can account for substantial variance. There are apt to be good reasons one architect is able to charge significantly more than another.

The Agreement and the Architect's Fee

An architect's fee for a custom single-family residential project is usually significantly higher than what the same architect would charge for commercial or institutional work. Clients bring a more complicated set of expectations and budget parameters to the project of building or remodeling their own houses. There are significantly more choices and complexities in custom residential work than in commercial projects.

Additional Costs

In addition to the architect's fees, you may incur additional costs for the services of professional consultants and for expenses incurred by your architect in the interest of the project. In general, any services not included under the descriptions of an architect's basic services are considered additional services and have a separate method for compensation. Most projects are completed without an architect undertaking any additional services, but any change in the scope or schedule of the project that requires the architect to invest time beyond what was described in the agreement could present a valid reason for additional compensation.

Most standard agreement forms include normal structural, mechanical, plumbing, heating, air-conditioning, and electrical engineering services in the architect's fee for basic services. However, some residential projects have unique site conditions, such as steep slopes, or are subject to extraordinary natural forces like hurricanes or earthquakes. Other projects necessitate special mechanical engineering requirements, such as elaborate lighting control systems or alternative energy sources—like ground-source heat pumps or solar collectors—that may require your architect to engage specialized engineering consultants. The cost for these professional services may not be included under the architect's basic services.

Reimbursable expenses, including costs for transportation, postage, and the reproduction of drawings and other documents, should be described in the agreement in addition to any multiplier or handling charges that may be applied to the actual cost incurred. Although these expenses are typically modest in relation to the overall fee, the costs associated with out-of-town travel can be significant, and procedures for authorizing such expenses should also be spelled out in the agreement.

Circumstances in which an architect would incur travel expenses could occur when the architect's firm and the client's project are in different cities or when the client and architect travel out-of-town together to visit a material supplier or showroom.

Most agreements also have an expiration date beyond which the architect can charge additional fees. Your architect presumes ongoing

Constructed as a temporary installation in 1999, the original apartment was intended to overlook the confluence of Pittsburgh's three rivers.

This view from the dining cove illustrates Wright's mastery of spatial relationships.

and methodical progress towards the fruition of your project and the completion of professional services. If you expect a delay in the project, to secure financing or for other reasons, it is good to discuss these factors with your architect in your earliest meetings so that any schedule contingencies can be incorporated into your agreement.

Invoices

Your agreement should describe how and when the architect will invoice for services and reimbursable expenses. It is fairly common for architects to submit their bills on a monthly basis. Some agreements afford you a thirty-day grace period to pay without penalty or interest. Also common in many agreements is a stipulation for an initial payment or retainer. These monies are paid to the architect upon execution of the agreement and credited to the owner's account at the time of final payment. In addition to a clear indication of good faith, the initial payment serves to compensate the architect during the lag between the time services are rendered and payment is received, as invoices typically are sent thirty days after services have been performed.

My firm customarily produces an invoicing schedule built upon the project timeline at the start of a project, so our clients have a clear understanding of their obligations and can arrange their finances accordingly. As will be detailed in the next chapter, the largest

investment of an architect's time in a project takes place after several months of design work, when he or she produces the construction documents. The amount of monthly invoicing increases in proportion.

Failed Agreements

Few couples going to the altar expect their marriage to end in divorce, and no one acting in good faith begins work with an architect on a residential project with anything but the sincerest expectations that the project will come to fruition in the form of a beautiful new or remodeled house. Those best intentions notwithstanding, your agreement for architectural services, as with any good prenuptial agreement, should clearly describe the terms for ending the relationship—what I've come to refer to in my discussions with clients as "the divorce clause." A good portion of most standard agreements describes the procedures for handling disputes between the parties should the need arise. Although fairly standard, these are aspects of the agreement that have definite legal consequences and may warrant the benefit of legal counsel.

One of the goals of this book is to reduce the potential for a failed "marriage" by eliminating the potential for misunderstanding. There are often other factors that necessitate contract termination, however. Many residential projects conceived by way of the best relationships fail to come to term for reasons unrelated to the

The Agreement and the Architect's Fee

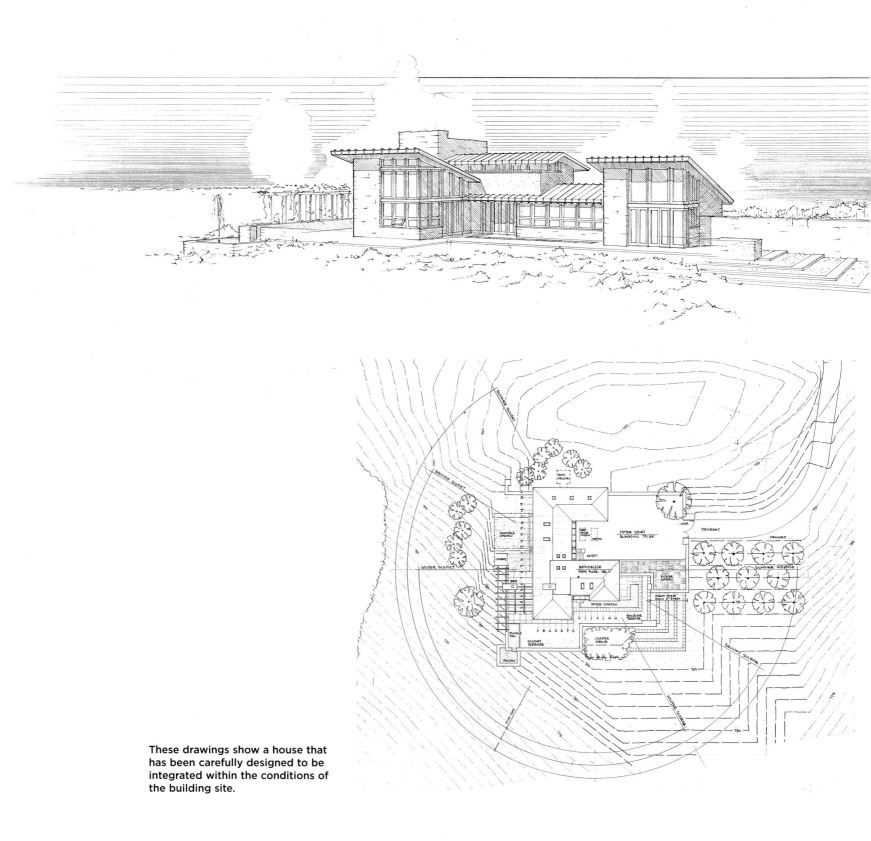

These drawings show a house that has been carefully designed to be integrated within the conditions of the building site.

actions of either the architect or client. Obstacles include the loss of a job, death, illness, injury, divorce, marriage, or work transfers. Fluctuations in the stock market, as well as natural and unnatural disasters, can also pose problems.

In such instances, it is good to note that the AIA standard form agreements and others afford the client the ability to terminate a project "for the Owner's convenience and without cause." In most agreements, the only grounds for termination on the part of your architect are for nonpayment and, less commonly, for egregious behaviors. While a premature termination of the relationship is not something that you're considering at the outset, take time to fully understand exactly what costs you will incur if you must end a project prematurely. The next chapter introduces the six steps to a successful project.

The Modernism of Richard Neutra

Richard Neutra is considered one of modernism's most important architects. Modernists apply scientific and analytical methods to design. Neutra's domestic architecture is a blend of art, landscape, and practical comfort. He is famous for the great attention he gave to defining the real needs of his clients.[1]

In 1936, Mr. and Mrs. John Nicholas Brown commissioned Neutra to translate their active interest in modernism into a custom-designed home at Fishers Island, New York. Mr. Brown, a member of one of America's oldest and most influential families, was a founding trustee of the Harvard Society of Contemporary Art and a member of the junior advisory committee of the newly founded Museum of Modern Art. When Neutra asked the couple for a description of their habits, lifestyle, and ideas for the house, they composed a seven-page memorandum providing insights into their everyday lives and a precise list of functions that the home should fulfill. This marked the beginning of one of the most enthralling dialogues of the twentieth century, and it epitomizes the value of communication between architect and client. Unfortunately, Windshield, the home Neutra built for the Browns, was destroyed by fire on New Year's Eve in 1973.[2]

[1] Thomas Hines, *Richard Neutra and the Search for Modern Architecture* (New York: Oxford University Press, 1982).

[2] Harvard University Art Museum Press Release (Cambridge: President and Fellows of Harvard College, 2003).

An alcove bar and sitting room resulted from the careful re-crafting of the spaces in this Dutch Colonial Revival house.

THE SIX PHASES OF WORKING WITH

an Architect

"The best clients are involved and critical. They are intelligent, reaching for something and not satisfied with the mediocre or offhand response. In the best work, we form a relationship that continues after the work is done. We have gained a measure of mutual respect."

—William (Bill) Dutcher, FAIA

Six Steps to a Successful Project

Working with an architect on a typical residential project usually involves six phases in sequence, although some architects combine several steps or add steps. As discussed in the last chapter, the written agreement with your architect should describe the services to be performed in each phase. The six phases are:

1. **Programming (Pre-Design Services):** deciding what to build and establishing a budget
2. **Schematic Design:** formulating the initial design solution
3. **Design Development:** developing and refining the design solution
4. **Construction Documents:** documenting the design in drawings and specifications
5. **Bidding or Negotiation:** selecting the contractor
6. **Construction or Construction Administration:** building the project

This remodeled kitchen represents a contemporary interpretation of materials and forms appropriate to the Dutch Colonial Revival house.

Programming Phase

You will accomplish much of the work of establishing a program before you begin looking for an architect. Your program is actually the "problem" for which an architect will work with you to develop a "solution." You may require additional space to accommodate a growing family or you may want a new kitchen. Your program is your wish list of wants and needs—an explanation of why you would like to build or remodel a house in the first place.

During the initial interview, the architect is likely to ask detailed questions about your requirements for the project (design objectives, limitations, and other criteria), your budget (available funds and financing considerations), and your schedule (critical dates that might impact the schedule, such as the birth of a child or graduation reception). The architect will use your responses to assess the reasonableness of your expectations. Before beginning any design work, your architect will test the fit between the key parts of the project—program, budget, and schedule—and recommend adjustments to assure a successful project. During this preliminary phase, your architect might also assist you in obtaining proposals for detailed land surveys for projects involving alterations and additions to an

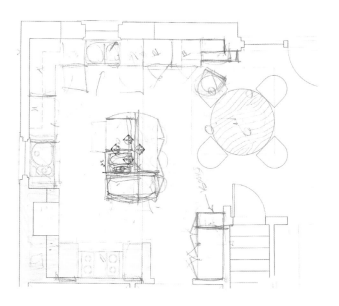

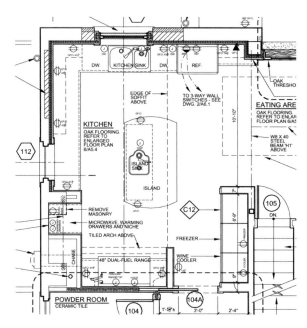

The layout of the kitchen is illustrated in the architect's design development sketch and construction drawing floor plans.

existing house or in making measured drawings of an existing structure.

Determining the Construction Budget

Your architect might consider the formula *Quantity x Quality = Cost,* or some variation of it, when determining a budget for your project. However explained, this formula remains the beginning and ending point of each and every architectural project. As the client, you determine two of the variables, and your architect will complete the equation. For example, if you want a 4,500-square-foot house with exotic interior finishes and a copper roof, the construction cost will be quite high. If your construction budget for the house is only $100,000, then your dream home may be more suitably scaled to be an exquisite children's playhouse.

Contrary to popular myth, architects, like most creative persons, achieve their best design solutions *within* a set of well-established parameters. As the client, you bring the essential ingredients of program, budget, and schedule from which your architect will create a design solution.

Establish your budget at the very beginning of the process—both the ideal and the maximum amount you are willing to spend. Clearly communicate this amount to your architect. Resist the temptation to withhold budget information from your architect by stating a budget that is lower or higher than what you are actually willing or able to spend. Everyone has a dollar figure that they are uncomfortable, or financially incapable of, exceeding. Your architect can

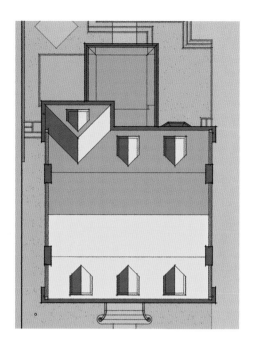

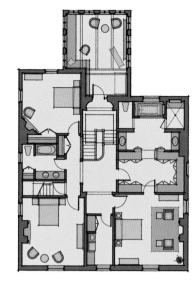

Plans for the first (middle) and second (right) floors of the Dutch Colonial Revival house show the relationships of the depicted spaces.

help you determine a realistic budget amount based on the project size, quality, and other criteria.

It is all too common for architects and owners to speak past each other when discussing an initial project budget. Many owners fail to account for the numerous hidden and additional costs that comprise a total project budget, and many architects tend to think of budgets solely in terms of a construction budget (the cost of the building itself). The sample budget worksheet on the facing page will help you estimate the costs involved in your project. You should complete this with your architect so you will both have an understanding of a construction budget that is appropriate for the project and in keeping with your particular financial circumstances. Keep in mind, however, that the costs

for a residential project remain indefinite, to some degree, until the very last bill from the contractor is paid. Building or remodeling a house is a far less tangible purchase than an automobile sitting fully assembled on the lot with a sticker price clearly printed in the window.

Making changes during construction, or even during the Construction Documents Phase after all the design decisions have been made, can be very expensive—many times more than if the same decisions had been incorporated into the project at the design phase. It is far easier to erase a line than to remove a wall. Your architect and builder can help you to make informed decisions about the cost and potential value of elements of your project during the early phases of your work together.

Budget Worksheet

LAND AND BUILDING ACQUISITION
Cost of buying land
Cost of buying a house
Title Report
Real estate appraisal
Financing costs, loan fees
Bonds and assessments
Legal fees (re-zoning, variances, and so on)
Topographic and boundary survey
Soils/geotechnical analysis/report
      Subtotal $_____

DESIGN
Architect's Fees
      Basic Services
      Existing conditions survey/documents
      Reimbursable expenses
      Additional services
      Models, 3-D renderings
Professional engineering fees
Professional landscape design fees
Interior design fees
Special engineering fees
      (solar, acoustical, and so on)
      Subtotal $_____

CONSTRUCTION
Detailed cost estimating
Site work
      Grading
      Utilities
      Road, driveway, paving

Building construction
Landscaping, planting, irrigation
Recreation features (swimming pool, tennis court)
Permit fees/construction taxes required by various
  public agencies
Insurance (builder's or owner's risk)
Materials testing and inspection
Built-in furniture and cabinetry
Audio, visual, computer equipment and wiring
Security system
      Subtotal $_____

FURNISHINGS
Specialty finishes
Flooring, carpeting, rugs
Interior furnishings and upholstery
Outdoor furnishings and accessories
Window coverings
Appliances
Fine art and decorative objects
      Subtotal $_____

OTHER
Construction contingency for variances in
  estimating and unforeseen expenses
Client contingency (to cover changes you make)
Adjustment for inflation
Cost of temporary lodging (if required)
Cost of temporary storage (if required)
Cost of delays
      Subtotal $_____

          TOTAL $_____

Cost Control

You've probably heard a horror story or two about an architect exceeding a client's budget by a large margin. Of course, the clients in many of those stories could not be more satisfied with the outcome of their projects. There are other projects, though, where the cost of the project so exceeds a client's budget that the house simply cannot be built as designed.

One of the best ways to avoid this kind of bitter disappointment is to acknowledge at the outset that neither you nor your architect can determine the actual cost of the labor, materials, and equipment for your project down to the penny. Nor can either of you control the contractor's methods of determining prices or market conditions that can drive up the costs of basic building materials by 200 percent or more in the weeks following a natural disaster in some other part of the country.

No architect can guarantee that the cost of a custom residential project will not exceed a stated budget, and it would be uncommon for an architect to agree to a fixed limit for the construction cost. In those instances when an architect does, you should expect to allow substantial contingencies for design, bidding, and price escalation. You should also afford a great deal of latitude in determining the materials, equipment, and types of construction to be used.

A view of the restored dining room looking into the living room in the Dutch Colonial Revival house.

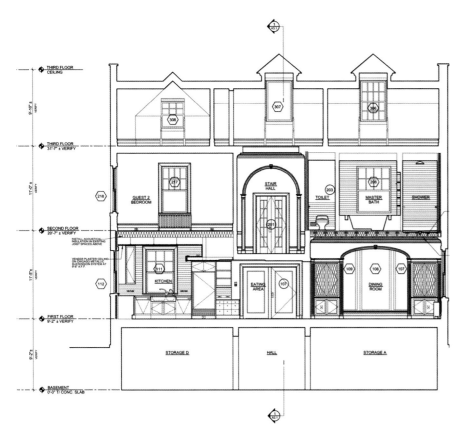

A vertical cross section through the entire Dutch Colonial Revival house.

In most instances, a custom residential project—be it a new house or alterations or additions to an existing home—is a singular, one-of-a-kind design solution. Although most projects share common elements, such as roofs, windows, walls, and floors, there is an almost infinite number of material and assembly choices for every element. The economies of scale common to the repetitive assembly of even the most exclusive and exotic automobiles are virtually nonexistent in the one-at-a-time construction process of building houses, a reality that makes it difficult for architects to detail the exact costs of the homes they design.

Despite the difficulties of establishing a fixed limit for the cost of a project, your architect should be able to prepare a good estimate of probable cost based upon volume or area calculations from recent projects. When you are interviewing architects, it would be good to inquire about their experience and track record in estimating costs. The standard agreement form calls for the architect to prepare initial statements of probable cost and to continually refine and recalculate these as the project progresses.

While it is all but impossible to guarantee that a design will not exceed a budget, you and your architect can agree on what to do if it does and make this a part of your written agreement. Standard AIA forms offer four remedies if the costs for a project come in over budget:

1. You can increase your budget.
2. You can try to achieve a lower cost by rebidding or soliciting additional proposals from contractors.
3. You can work with your architect to reduce the scope and/or quality of the project.
4. You can terminate the contract with your architect.

These options are all fairly radical, offering variations on a theme of disappointment. Any of these choices is all but certain to leave you and your architect wishing you had never met. Seeking to avoid this kind of disappointment and to remove much of the cost uncertainty inherent in residential projects, many architects bring a contractor into the mix during the early stages of the design process.

During the building boom of the bull market of the 1990s, it became virtually impossible to solicit competitive bids from qualified residential contractors. The best contractors enjoyed a long waiting list of potential clients. They were too busy to invest the time required to prepare a competitive bid on projects against three other contractors when they might have only a 25 percent chance of receiving the job. In response to this dearth of potential bidders, many architects began to explore negotiated contracts for the construction of their client's projects. Other architects, in states where it is not prohibited, entered into business relationships with contractors to offer a hybrid service called design-build, whereby owners contract with a single entity for both the design and construction of their project. Both of these approaches, as well as the traditional bidding method, are discussed in detail later in this chapter.

Schedule

It is important to be entirely honest with your architect about your expectations for the schedule of your project. Taking into consideration the scope and scale of your project, as well

Ludwig Mies van der Rohe

Ludwig Mies van der Rohe, a proponent of the utopian International Style and famous for his dictum *less is more,* was dedicated to his vision of skin-and-bones minimalist architecture. His most famous residential project, and one of only three still standing, was the 1951 Farnsworth House, in Plano, Illinois. The house is exquisitely simple and beautiful as an abstract statement.

As the house neared completion, Mies's friendship with his client, Dr. Edith Farnsworth, broke up. The extremely unpleasant aftermath involved lawsuits (decided in Mies's favor), recriminations in public and private on the part of Dr. Farnsworth, and denunciations of Mies as a menace to American architecture. This latter campaign took the form of a concerted attack in the pages of the Hearst magazine *House Beautiful,* in which Dr. Farnsworth expressed her dissatisfaction and disappointment with the project.[1] Today, the Farnsworth House is owned by the National Trust for Historic Preservation and can be toured.

[1] Peter Blake, *Mies van der Rohe: Architecture and Structure* (New York: Alfred A. Knopf, 1964).

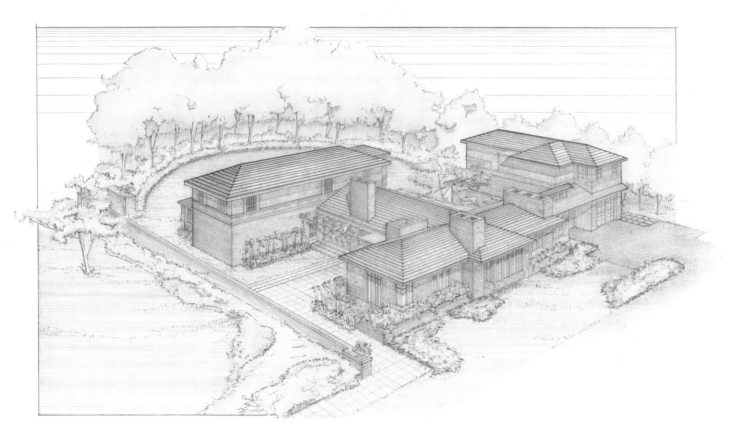

Color pencil drawing showing aerial perspective view of extensive remodeling and additions to a 1950s ranch house.

as his or her other obligations, your architect can determine if your plans are realistic. Like clockwork, every March my office fields some half dozen calls from potential clients who are poised to begin a major remodeling project with the goal of occupying the result by Thanksgiving. And, invariably, I politely inquire, "You do mean Thanksgiving of *next* year?"

Certainly you should advise your architect if you have a major social event in the works for which you expect your project to be complete. Major events like an upcoming wedding can introduce a great deal of personal stress and anxiety into a project, but nothing can be more challenging to the successful delivery of a project than the birth of a child. The burden

of carrying both a child and an architectural project to term can overcome even the most stalwart of couples. Expectant parents would be well advised not to schedule the delivery of both projects around the same time.

Take time to plan for your project, allowing your architect and contractor the time needed to properly design and build your project. Blocking out a preliminary schedule on a calendar can be informative for everyone involved and can help limit the possibility of disappointment. Depending on the scope and scale of the project and on your availability, you should allow three to six months for the initial design phases of the project. Larger projects may take upwards of a year to plan and complete the construction documents. Based on his or her prior experience, your architect should be able to advise you regarding the time required for the actual construction. In general, projects of any complexity cannot be brought to final completion by a contractor in less than ninety days, and major renovations or the construction of a new house from the ground up can take anywhere from nine to eighteen months—longer if, for example, weather or unforeseen delays become factors.

There are some twenty luxury co-op buildings in Manhattan, including 927 Fifth Avenue and 730 Park Avenue, where construction is strictly limited to the time between Memorial Day and Labor Day, and come September, incomplete work is suspended until the following spring.[2] This extreme example underscores the added value of establishing a relationship with a contractor early in the design process.

Schematic Design Phase

You've found *your* architect. You have carefully negotiated and executed a written agreement. You have worked together to achieve a mutual understanding of your program, budget, and schedule. A survey of your property or drawings of the existing conditions of your home are in hand. Your financing is in the works. At last, you're ready for the really fun part—the design solution.

[2] Christopher Mason, "In August, The Rich Race to Renovate," The *New York Times*, 25 August 2005.

Typical Distribution of an Architect's Fee

Although the percentages will vary slightly depending on your project and how your architect distributes his or her time, the following breakdown represents the typical distribution of an architect's total basic services fee for most residential projects:

Phase	% of Total Fee
• **Programming and Schematic Design Phases**	15%
• **Design Development Phase**	20%
• **Construction Documents Phase**	40%
• **Bidding Phase**	5%
• **Construction Phase**	20%
TOTAL	100%

Remember that additional services, as defined in your agreement, as well as your architect's reimbursable expenses will be in addition to the total fee for basic services.

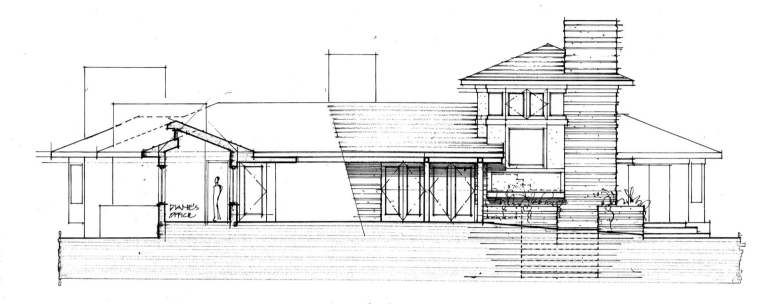

A partial section and elevation illustrate key spatial relationships in this Design Development drawing of the ranch house.

The conception of a design solution is perhaps the most exhilarating, enchanting, and magical time in a client-architect relationship. Architects are inculcated with the significance of this initial act from the outset of their professional education. The best of them come to understand that the larger responsibilities of the relationship are only beginning.

I consider my ability to conceive a design solution appropriate to the needs of my clients to be my greatest skill; it's the reason I was compelled to pursue this vocation from a young age. Yet, after years of practice and scores of clients, I continue to marvel at the essential leap of faith taken by clients as they entrust their hopes for a three-dimensional realization of their needs, wants, and desires, conceived in concert with the requirements of their site and budget, into my hands.

During the Schematic Design Phase, your architect will produce a schematic, or conceptual, design that establishes the scale and relationship of components of the design solution (e.g., the arrangement of rooms and the general organization of the site). Your architect will also review alternative approaches to design and construction with you. The Schematic Design Phase typically comprises 10 to 15 percent of an architect's total compensation. Every architect has a design methodology and presentation style unique to his or her practice. You should have gotten a pretty clear idea of what to expect from your architect in terms of process and physical presentation of materials as a result of discussions during your initial interview, as well as from the terms of your agreement.

I personally eschew the practice where, after the initial programming meetings, the architect makes a lavish presentation of elaborately rendered and fully developed design drawings. While this makes for high drama, it can also result in unpleasant surprise and disappointment for both client and architect, particularly if the architect's vision is inconsistent with the client's needs or preferences. There is a reason that appetizers are commonly served before the main course.

Although a design solution often becomes apparent to me early in the relationship (sometimes even at the initial meeting), I have found the process of working with my clients to be much more rewarding and ultimately more productive when I engage clients in the incremental development of a design solution. This can be as informal as an initial sketch on tracing paper over the plans of their existing home or a series of small-scale floor plan options loosely rendered in a graphic format on the computer. Though there are many appropriate ways to work through this conceptual phase, the most important thing is that you and your architect have a mutual understanding of your expectations.

The drawings in this phase might include a conceptual site plan, if appropriate, as well as preliminary building plans, sections, and elevations. Your architect may also choose to include study models or perspective sketches. It is not uncommon today for some architects to electronically compose three-dimensional models, static renderings, or animations to visually walk you through the conceptual space. If your architect suggests that a model or computer rendering might be helpful to the process, be certain to determine if this additional work, which could be substantial, is included in the basic fee.

Together with drawings and other presentation materials, your architect should prepare a preliminary estimate of construction costs. In this initial phase, an estimate is based on area, volume, or similar conceptual estimating techniques. As many details remain to be established, it is very difficult for your architect to make an accurate determination of costs. You should expect to see a large contingency or range of probable costs to account for the changes in cost that will invariably occur as the design is further developed.

In many projects, a range of options may be explored during this initial phase. You may not have a clear idea of what is possible or, based upon the possible options, a clear sense of what monies you might be willing to invest. Using the example of a kitchen remodeling, this phase could be utilized to evaluate the difference in design and cost between a solution that occupied only the interior space of an existing kitchen compared to a scheme that would incorporate the construction of a new addition.

Remember throughout the design process that this is, after all, *your* home. However, be flexible about achieving the design solution. Sometimes the best solution is arrived at through a process of sketching, discussions, and revisions

Art and architecture: this art-glass mural graces the elevator lobby entry to a condominium apartment.

that can take time. In the best relationship, an architect will work closely with you to give form to your ideas. Your acceptance of a final version of your architect's schematic design efforts, and a corresponding preliminary estimate of the cost of work, will signify the conclusion of the Schematic Design Phase. Your acceptance should be recorded in writing. To avoid any potential for misunderstanding, you might also sign or initial the drawings that represent your accepted scheme. This acceptance becomes the basis for the further development of the design in the next phase.

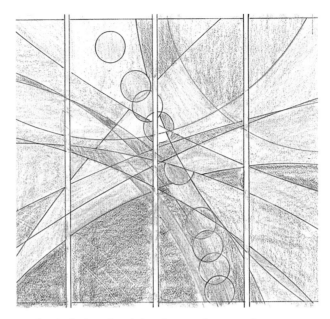

Author's design sketch for the art-glass panels.

Design Development Phase

During the Design Development Phase, your architect will work with you to further develop and refine, and more fully describe the size and character of, your project. Your architect will identify building materials; structural, mechanical, and electrical systems; and just about every other element that will be incorporated into the construction of your project, right down to the doorbell. This phase accounts for a significant portion of a typical fee—about 20 to 25 percent. It requires the most participation from you as the owner. This is also the phase of the project where the *quality* choices that can most affect the construction budget are considered. The participation of a contractor in the consideration of these choices can be invaluable in helping to keep costs within budget.

The work in this phase is based on the drawings and budget that you approved at the conclusion of the Schematic Design Phase. You may continue to make adjustments to the project requirements, schedule, or construction budget as your architect works to develop more detailed drawings and preliminary specifications. Do your best to make decisions in a timely manner. If you change your mind, tell your architect immediately. Endeavor not to revisit or reverse decisions that you already made because it is likely your architect already acted on them and thus significant changes could incur additional costs.

Although there can be variation, during design development your architect will normally begin to prepare the drawings and preliminary specifications that will become the final construction

Custom built-in furnishings contribute to the harmonious design throughout the space in this condominium apartment.

documents. The documents will become the basis of the contract with a builder for the construction of your project. In this phase, the documents should clearly illustrate and describe the design. The documents should also define the scope, relationships, forms, size, and appearance of the project by means of plans, sections, and elevations, typical construction details, and equipment layouts (see pages 86–87 for a description of these terms). Finally, the specifications should establish the quality level for all major materials and systems.

The Design Development Phase can be quite taxing for you the client because of the sheer number of choices to consider and decisions to make. You will need to make decisions about ceiling, wall, and floor finishes; lighting and lighting controls; bathroom fixtures, fittings, and accessories; kitchen appliances, fixtures, finishes, and accessories; decorative and other hardware; and more. Even a small kitchen remodeling involves hundreds of options from which you must make selections.

You may be comfortable to defer to the judgment of your architect and builder on some of the decisions regarding major building components like roofing material and the style of the windows and doors. Your architect or builder can also provide advice on everything from the ingredients for the concrete in the foundations to the type of screws to be utilized for the installation of the drywall.

Your ability to consider all the choices and to make timely selections depends largely on your personality, disposition, and available time. Don't allow your architect or builder to rush you into making hasty decisions, but take care not to unduly procrastinate either.

I occasionally have clients who afford me carte blanche to make all the detailed selections for their homes. Just as infrequently, I have clients at the opposite extreme who become hopelessly lost in the glitter of a plumbing-fixture showroom, reducing themselves to tears over the seemingly unlimited number of choices.

As with the initial design concepts, architects work in different ways through the design development process. From your initial interview

An end table that is integral to the built-in seating unit also incorporates storage.

Furnishings along this condominium wall conceal three drop-leaf tables that can be combined for large dinner parties.

you should have a clear understanding of exactly how your architect intends to work with you on these key decisions. The amount of time your architect will spend with you in considering these details, and the degree to which he or she will document the choices within the drawings and specifications, will be reflected in the fee. Many architects simply do not involve themselves with the selection and specification of the detail components of their projects. Some steadfastly remand their clients to a kitchen and bath showroom to make selections on their own or leave such detailed decisions for the clients to work out with their contractor.

It is the custom in my office to work with clients to select each and every element that goes into the final construction of their project—from the shingles on the roof down to the paper holder in the bathroom. This assures continuity in design appearance and overall quality, leaving nothing to chance. In general, I work to reduce the potential options to those selections that are appropriate to both the design and budget of the project. This all takes a great deal of time and energy. I break up the meetings through the Design Development Phase over several weeks or months, and treat each with an agenda specific to one particular area of the house at a time.

As noted previously, resist revisiting decisions once you make them. Every decision affects the work done after it. Changes can be costly. Your architect can establish a defined account of a stipulated sum from which you can later withdraw funds to pay for unselected elements in the project. Although decisions about cabinet knobs may appear to be discreet, these items tend to have unimaginably long lead times for delivery. It is always a good idea to make as many decisions as possible up front and incorporate them into the drawings and specifications at the outset.

At the completion of the Design Development Phase, you should have a fairly refined set of drawings that give a clear representation of the proposed design in detail, as well as an outline specification that identifies all the major materials and finishes. To keep the project moving, promptly review the drawings and materials your architect gives you and return them quickly with questions, comments, and changes. Your architect, possibly in cooperation with your builder, will make revisions that may be necessary to stay within the original estimate of the cost of the project. Based

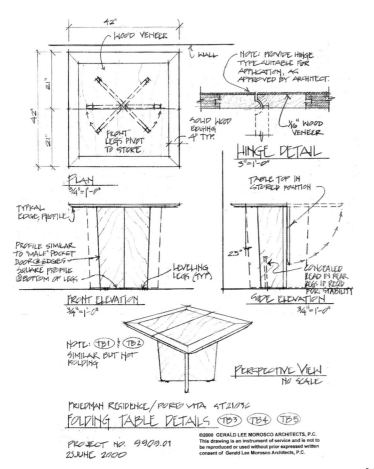

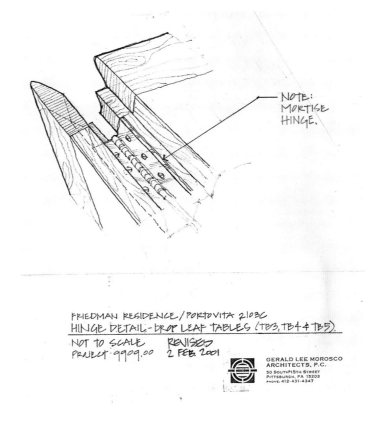

Two drawings illustrate the construction details for the custom drop-leaf tables.

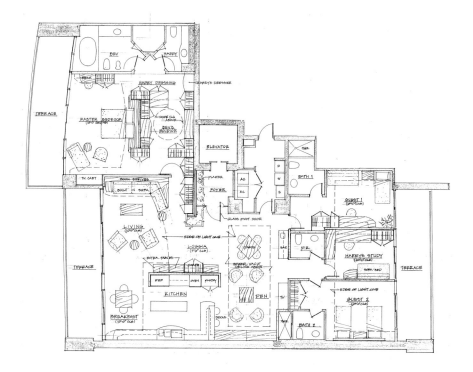

Preliminary floor plan illustrates the condominium in its entirety.

on your approval of these drawings, your architect will proceed to prepare the construction documents.

Construction Documents Phase

By the Construction Documents Phase, your work in helping to conceive and develop the design is largely complete. Yet this phase accounts for some 40 percent of a typical fee, since this is when most of the architect's work is undertaken. After your approval of the design development documents and any adjustments to the project in terms of scope, quality, or changes to your construction budget, your architect will prepare detailed drawings and specifications that the contractor can use to determine actual construction costs, obtain permits, and then actually build the project.

If you have requested changes from the Design Development Phase, perhaps relocating a door or adding a telephone jack, such changes should be represented in the final construction drawings. At times the unavailability of some material or component may also require a modification to the construction drawings and specifications.

The level of detail and completeness in a set of construction documents is one of the most tangible measures of an architect's value. These documents are typically detailed iterations of the design development drawings but bear little resemblance to the graphically more straightforward representations of the project depicted in these and the earlier schematic design drawings. The construction drawings will appear to be visually cluttered with string lines of dimensions, detailed notations, schedules, and graphic symbols; each of these elements conveys specific information to the builder in a kind of shorthand, mostly unintelligible to those outside the construction industry.

The construction documents are, in effect, the detailed assembly instructions for your custom-designed house or remodeling. Many projects employ time-tested and familiar construction and assemblies; others test the limits of new technologies. As the author of the design and the assembly instructions, your architect can serve as an important interpreter during construction. It is unlikely that any set of

Subtle barrel-vault ceiling and cove lighting expand the reality of the space in the den of the condominium apartment.

drawings and specifications will account for every contingency—particularly for projects that involve alterations to existing structures, where previously unseen conditions may require modifications during construction. This is but one important reason to retain the services of your architect through the entire construction process, as will be discussed later in this chapter.

In addition to preparing the drawings and specifications, your architect will work with you, your legal and insurance advisers, and your lender to establish the terms and conditions for the contract with the builder for the construction. Depending on the particular requirements of your project, these terms and conditions may address, for example, when and how the contactor will be paid and what percentage of each progress payment to the contractor will be retained. The lender may require certain inspections or approvals prior to release of final payment. Your attorney and insurer may

recommend specific requirements for the limits and coverage of the contractor's liability insurance as well as modifications to your own liability and property insurance during construction.

At this point, if you have not involved a contractor during the design phases, your architect can help you identify potential qualified bidders and assist you in the preparation of bidding documents, invitations to bid, and instructions to bidders.

Obviously, you must rely on your architect's professional skill and care for the preparation of these detailed construction documents on your behalf. As was the case with every step that preceded this, ask as many questions as necessary to be sure that you understand the information conveyed in the drawings. The completed construction documents will be used by the contractor to establish a final cost for the building and as the basis for your agreement to construct the project.

The Six Phases of Working with an Architect

Common Terms Used by Architects

Blueprints is an archaic reference from an earlier time when an architect's original velum or paper drawings were reproduced on photosensitive paper and developed with ammonia. Despite the fact that it has been well over fifty years since blueprints were actually dark blue sheets of paper with white lines, many architects and contractors continue to use this term or simply the term prints to refer to reproduced sets of the original drawings.

Also increasingly uncommon today are the results of a subsequent technology that produced blue lines on white paper. Reproductions are now commonly printed out on large printers and photocopiers as black lines on white paper.

Contract documents consist of the actual contract (agreement) between the owner and contractor for the construction of the project, the conditions for that agreement (sometimes these conditions are outlined in a separate document called the General Conditions), and the drawings and specifications.

Detail drawings are even closer depictions of selected assemblies and parts, such as windowsills or roof eaves. Drawings for very detailed trim pieces, like baseboards or decorative moldings, are sometimes drawn at full scale to clearly convey an architect's design intent.

Drawings can refer to the original documents or, synonymous with blueprints, to any reproductions. In our technologically advanced world of computer-aided drafting (CAD), an architect's original drawings often exist only as electronic files. The architect can reduce and enlarge the scale and "cut and paste" together a complete set of construction drawings.

There are several types of drawings that architects combine to convey information to the contractor. Drawings employ various graphic keys and notations to weave the drawings together in a well-established format common in the construction industry. Drawings are commonly printed at scale as accurately scaled-down representations of a full-size design. Notations that identify the drawing and scale are now commonly placed directly below each drawing on a sheet.

Elevation drawings are straight-on views of either the exterior walls of the building (facade) or of selected interior walls. These drawings illustrate the locations of doors and windows and the positions of electrical devices. Elevation drawings also give detailed information about wall finishes and decorative details.

Floor plan drawings are more detailed diagrammatic representations of each floor illustrating the size and relationship of the rooms and other spaces and including detailed dimensions. These drawings depict a horizontal slice through the building, and much like a CAT scan in medicine, illustrate the interior assemblies of the walls and other elements as cut sections as well. Typically the "cut" is made several feet above the floor so that the windows and doors can be illustrated in relation to the plan. Floor plan drawings can indicate the floor finishes as well. Floor plan drawings or specially annotated electrical plan drawings also identify the locations for electrical receptacles, telephone and data ports, and the like.

Foundation plan drawings establish the locations for the foundations, or footings, and can include the floor plan for a basement, if any.

Reflected ceiling plan drawings are the mirror image of floor plan drawings (imagine lying on the floor and looking up at the ceiling). These drawings show detailed ceiling elements as well as the location of recessed and decorative lighting fixtures. On a lighting plan, graphic lines tie a series of light fixtures together on a common circuit and connect them to a light switch. Take time to carefully "walk through" each of the spaces on the plans with your architect to get a clear understanding of how the furniture might be arranged and how you might live in the space. This visualization will help you to consider whether the placement of light switches and receptacles is effective.

Schedules are detailed lists referenced to the drawings that specify finishes, materials, and products.

A typical project might include schedules for room finishes; door, window, and other hardware; plumbing fixtures and fittings; and lighting fixtures. Specifications are commonly bound into a booklet, sometimes called a Project Manual, that is separate from the larger drawings. However, in their most abbreviated form, the specifications can be printed together with the drawings. While the drawings convey information to the contractor about quantity, dimension, and location, the specifications spell out the details of the construction materials and the methods and techniques for installation. These drawings can be so detailed as to identify every screw and nail for each application in the construction of the house by manufacturer and model number. Less detailed variants afford the contractor multiple choices that meet certain performance criteria.

Section drawings are more detailed views of horizontal or vertical slices through particular assemblies, such as footings, floors, walls, and roofs. They provide dimensions and identify the locations and relationships of building materials.

Site plan drawings establish the location of the building on the lot and frequently identify the property lines and the locations of utilities. These drawings also show driveways and other paved areas and include instructions for grading the land.

The sleek kitchen features a one-piece sink and hob unit designed by automotive-designer Pininfarina.

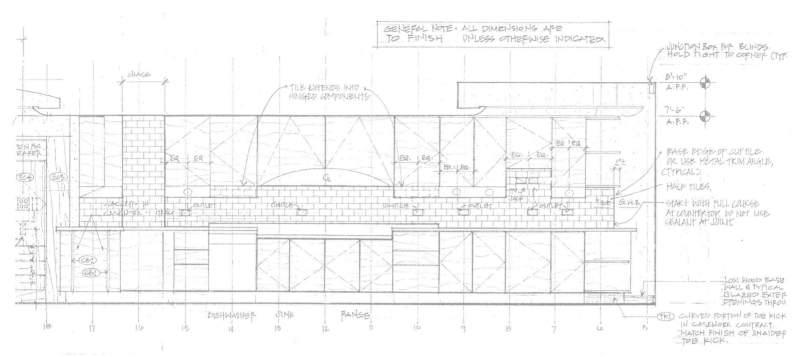

Elevation drawing that shows the
careful attention to detail given
to the kitchen backsplash tile.

Architects and Contractors

The distinction between architects and contractors is relatively recent in the history of
building. In Renaissance times, architects func-
tioned as master builders, designing projects
and directing the construction of projects. In
contrast, over the past hundred years or so,
there has been an increased complexity in
construction materials and methods, evident
in many of the features of our houses that we
now take for granted, like indoor plumbing
and electricity. The gap has widened between
the crafts of design and construction, and
specialization within each has increased. The
separation between architects and contractors
has also solidified as a result of the development of increasingly detailed building codes
and other regulations that governing authorities
employ to protect the health, safety, and welfare
of the public.

There are several potential approaches to the
construction of your project, each with advantages and disadvantages. Your architect can
advise you of which method is most appropriate
for the particular circumstances of your project.

The Contractor's Role

The majority of custom-home construction
involves a general contractor in some capacity.
A general contractor brings the various parts
of the composition together at precisely the
right time and in the most logical and economical sequence. Contractors may complete
concrete and masonry work, drywall and plas-
tering, painting, or roofing themselves. In most
instances, they hire subcontractors to accomplish those trades that they themselves do not
"self-perform," often things like plumbing,
electrical work, and heating and air-conditioning. Contractors charge for work they

The Six Phases of Working with an Architect

self-perform and for the superintendence of the subcontractors in addition to some percentage of the aggregate amount of all the subcontracts. Contractors calculate their fees in almost as many different ways as do architects. The markup on a project can range from 10 percent to more than 20 percent. Depending on the size of the company, the contractor may take on only one project at a time or may have multiple crews working on several projects simultaneously.

I caution you to choose a general contractor with even more care than you gave to the selection of your architect. While the same kinds of questions and considerations apply, the contractor will be responsible for the physical delivery of that which you and your architect have so carefully conceived.

Your architect may have past experience with several contractors, and he or she may be able to give you some assurances as to the professional capability of each of them. In lieu of direct past experience, your architect can make a visual evaluation of the completed work of several contractors and can speak with other architects about their experiences with prospective contractors. It is best for you to find out from other owners just how the contractors and their crews were as houseguests. Did they wipe their feet before they walked across the living room carpet? Indeed, in the case of a remodeling

project, this is the person whose crew will arrive to begin hammering away at seven in the morning.

Acting as Your Own Contractor

It is not uncommon for owners to look for additional savings by acting as their own general contractors. Given the right circumstances, this approach can be plausible and successful. It does, however, create a significant imbalance in the traditional relationship between a client and an architect. Most of the standard agreement forms do not anticipate this arrangement. If you would like to consider acting as your own contractor, you should discuss this with your architect at the outset.

My best advice to my clients comes by way of my own example. As an apprentice at Taliesin, I gained significant hands-on experience on actual projects in the drafting studio as well as by participating in construction. Acting as general contractor and laborer, my experience at Taliesin culminated in the construction of the building that houses the Frank Lloyd Wright Archives at Taliesin West. Despite my experience, when the time came for the construction of my own home in Pittsburgh, conveniently located directly across the street from my architectural practice, I eschewed the role of general contractor though it was within my reach. The argument by which I persuaded myself, and that I have made successfully to all of my clients, is that you will be able to earn far more by continuing to devote your energies to your vocation than you could ever hope to save by acting as your own general contractor.

Bidding or Negotiation Phase

By tradition, the most common method by which architects and contractors deliver their services is through separate contracts. An owner first contracts with an architect and, through the process described in this book, works with the architect to achieve a design solution that the architect subsequently depicts in a detailed set of construction documents. The architect assists the owner in obtaining either competitive bids or negotiated proposals from contractors. The architect then helps the client select the contractor most appropriate for the project and then prepares the contract for construction with the contractor.

Soliciting Competitive Bids from Contractors

Traditionally, one of the advantages of having an architect prepare a detailed set of drawings and specifications has been that the owner can solicit competitive bids and, presumably, obtain the best price for the work. This method of securing a contractor is well established in many public projects when very stringent requirements surround the bidding process. Unless otherwise disqualified, the low bidder is normally awarded the contract. In private work, however, the owner customarily reserves the right to reject all bids. Even when the bid amounts are close to the budget,

owners frequently endeavor to negotiate a lower price with a selected bidder.

As I wrote earlier in this chapter, I have found it increasingly difficult, if not impossible, to engage the most highly qualified residential contractors in competitive bidding for a residential project because they have sufficient work already. My experience has also confirmed that competitive bidding does not necessarily yield the lowest price for carefully specified work—it simply reveals the best price among a certain number of contractors at a fixed point in time. For instance, if a contractor is bidding against three other contractors for a project, he or she has only a 25 percent chance of securing that contract. Bids also do not always represent the actual cost of the work. In a two-to-four-week bidding period, the contractor is expected to become intimately familiar with a set of detailed documents and then copy and distribute those documents to obtain prices from subcontractors and suppliers. During the time the contractor is preparing to bid on your job, he or she may also be bidding on several projects and directing ongoing construction on others. Residential contractors usually have very few, if any, administrative support personnel, and the same is true for the majority of their subcontractors.

Given these constraints, most residential contractors must pad their numbers to account for

In this master bedroom, all necessities are within reach.
The television is concealed in the footboard cabinet.

things they may have missed in the drawings, missing or incomplete bids from subcontractors, and a host of other contingencies. If they are successful in securing the contract, they will endeavor to secure the most favorable pricing from their suppliers so they can deliver the project for their bid price or even a lower price, which obviously would increase their profit. This process is further flawed in that the low bidder may have critically under-estimated the cost to do the work and subsequently may be unable to take on the job. Or the contractor may win another job during the bidding period and be unavailable to start your project as planned.

A Negotiated Agreement with a Contractor
Involving a contractor during the initial design development phase of a project offers several clear advantages over soliciting bids. It also helps you avoid what is perhaps the single largest threat to the relationship between a client and architect: construction bids that come in significantly over budget. Here are some other advantages to working with a contractor from the beginning:

• Most importantly, you can negotiate a cost-plus contract (the actual cost of the materials plus an agreed-upon percentage markup for the contractor), with or without a guaranteed maximum price, so that you will know exactly what the cost of your project will be.
• A general contractor can work with you and your architect during the development of the design solution to consider materials and construction assemblies that will work within your budget.
• You will eliminate the uncertainty of having to wait until a contractor is available, which will give you the opportunity to schedule the work to begin at a time that is convenient for both of you.
• Subcontractors are more willing to offer detailed bids for their work when they know that the contactor has secured the job.
• Once under agreement, the contractor can place orders for long-lead items, such as custom windows and doors and specialty materials. The extra time also affords an opportunity for the contractor to be more strategic in buying materials with price volatility.

My experience has been that involving the contractor early in the process with a negotiated contract for construction is the fairest and most economical way to undertake residential projects. Typically, the general contractor competitively bids all of the major subcontracts. At the outset of the relationship, the contractor's fee for services, as well as the rate for overhead and profit, are negotiated and stipulated within the agreement.

A small portion, generally about 5 percent, of your architect's total compensation will be allocated to the bidding and negotiation. If a contractor is secured early in the project, this portion of the fee may be distributed through the phases preceding construction. If you elect to solicit bids for the project this portion will occur discreetly between the completion of the Construction Documents Phase and the beginning of construction.

Design-Build Construction

A design-build arrangement harks back to the days of architect as master builder. Some states prohibit architects from offering construction services, finding such arrangements to be in conflict with existing professional licensure laws that were crafted to secure the architect in the role of representing the client's interests with the contractor during construction. However, this design-build method of project delivery has become increasingly common, and changes in existing statutes have made it entirely legal in many parts of the country.

In many instances, custom homebuilders have added architects to their staff. Offering a single point of project responsibility, these so-called design-build companies offer a seamless process from start to finish. Unlike custom homebuilders, where the architect, if there is one, is likely to be working in a back room, design-build firms market professional architect services as an integral part of the process, and clients are typically involved with the

architect from start to finish. Similarly, architectural firms, seeking to achieve greater control over the construction process and a better understanding of construction costs, have established relationships with builders to create design-build firms. Many architects maintain their traditional architectural practices as well.

You might have less control over the design process under the design-build arrangement. When design-build firms accept the responsibility of designing a project with a fixed budget and schedule, they frequently assume control of any decisions that might affect their ability to keep the project within budget or on schedule. On the plus side, there could be some cost savings associated with design-build, but you might want to compare the price and work with that of independent architects and contractors before making a final decision.

Given that design-build is an all-or-nothing relationship, you should use the utmost care in selecting a firm. Become familiar with exactly how the design process will work, how compensation and payment will be determined, and what the terms and conditions stipulate if the relationship is unsuccessful.

Construction Phase

Whether you secure a contractor by way of negotiation or through competitive bidding,

Here the ceiling cove is orchestrated to lead one's eye to the view of the ocean beyond.

Space for this commodious powder room in the
Dutch Colonial Revival House pictured at the beginning of
this chapter was captured from a former service stair.

your architect will assist you in awarding the contract to the builder and in preparing the contract for construction. The AIA publishes a number of agreements for various types of projects that dovetail together with the AIA owner-architect agreements that are commonly used by architects and contractors. Should you utilize nonstandard or customized agreements, it is important that roles and responsibilities assigned to your architect are consistent in both the owner-client and owner-contractor agreements.

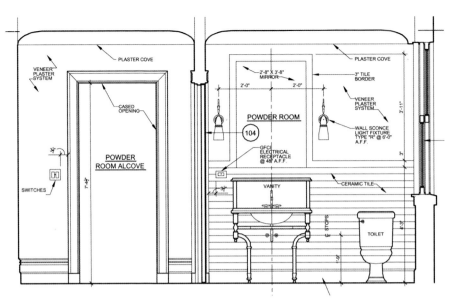

Interior elevation of the Dutch Colonial Revival House from the construction drawings delineates the placement of every element in the powder room.

Most of the standard owner-contractor agreements incorporate a set of general conditions. In a residential project, conditions can run the gamut from mundane yet significant policies regarding the contractor's right to use your bathroom to more complex details about how the contractor must prepare and submit applications for payment. Conditions have evolved to account for the many contingencies inherent in even the largest construction projects. Obviously, a contract for the construction of a multimillion-dollar home would not be appropriate for a modest kitchen remodeling. Your architect, together with your legal counsel, can help you select an agreement form and general conditions appropriate to the scope and scale of your project. Take the time to review carefully and establish the conditions for your agreement with the contractor, as these will govern the important months of labor that lead up to the much

anticipated delivery of your completed project. The basic services of the typical owner-architect agreements call for the architect to function as your representative with the contractor during construction. Your architect will visit the construction site at appropriate intervals to observe the progress and overall quality of the work. Depending on the scope and detail of the project, your architect may arrange to have weekly or biweekly meetings with the contractor at the job site to review the progress and quality of the work. While the architect has the authority, as your representative, to reject work that does not conform to the contract documents and may authorize minor changes in the work, he or she cannot make any changes that would increase either the contract sum or time to complete the project.

If your project involves alterations or additions to your existing home and you are in residence,

The tiled niche reinforces the traditional detailing.

you will obviously be in a position to observe the work on a daily basis. If you notice anything questionable, you should not hesitate to communicate directly with your architect, *not* the contractor or subcontractors. Communication regarding the work of the contractor or subcontractors should always go through your architect.

Prior to the Construction Phase, your project had existed for you only as an abstract visualization in your mind's eye. Not even the best drawings, renderings, models, or most realistic computer animations can prepare you for the emotional roller coaster of seeing the project transform through its various three-dimensional manifestations. From the initial layout lines on the ground, to the completion of the rough

A traditional tiled alcove enframes the state-of-the-art soaking tub in the second-floor bathroom of the Dutch Revival House.

One half of a matched set of his-and-her vanities in the Dutch Colonial Revival house.

framing, to the closing in with sheathing, to the addition of the drywall, you might alternately perceive the project as too large or too small, depending on when you observe it. I often remind clients who are in the midst of an anxious moment that this is why surgeons use anesthesia during surgical procedures. Your architect will reassure you that the project will eventually assume a form that you recognize as that which you conceived together so many months ago.

The Tale of the $500 Electrical Outlet

Once upon a time, there was an architect's client who, spending most of the day at home, developed a rapport with the workers constructing an addition to her kitchen. One day, the owner noticed one of the workers installing electrical outlets. The friendly woman asked, "Do you think you could install an extra outlet over there, too?" Feeling that the owner had directed him, the responsible worker smiled and obliged. He stayed late that night to install the outlet before the drywall subcontractor arrived the next morning. As he should, the worker submitted his overtime for the extra outlet to his boss, who added the nominal cost of the outlet and wire, applied the appropriate markup, and submitted a bill to the general contractor, who marked it up again and submitted it to the architect as a change order authorized by the owner. When the architect presented the contractor's invoice for $500 to the owner, she exclaimed, "Oh! He didn't tell me it was going to cost anything. I thought he was just being courteous!"

Changes are part of almost every construction project, but they should be kept to a minimum. When necessary, there is a well-established process whereby your architect will solicit a proposal for the cost of a change from the contractor before the work is undertaken so that it can be agreed upon beforehand.

The bronze pulls on the cabinet doors in this early-twentieth-century Arts and Crafts home were custom cast from an original antique furniture pull from the client's collection.

Great?

"In all our work, we endeavor to distinguish the curious from the beautiful. This, as the true architect's calling, remains our greatest task."

—Gerald Lee Morosco, AIA

A Collaborative Effort

Residential architects are as many and varied as their clients. Each has his or her individual approach to design and method of working with clients. The most successful projects are born of an effort on the part of the architect and client to maintain clear and open communication. This effort must begin with that very first date, which I've talked about throughout this book, and be sustained through the conception, labor, and delivery of the project.

Even those architects who have well-established reputations for exceptional design, attention to detail, and excellence in project execution can falter in a relationship with a client.

Unreasonable expectations brought about by a client's fundamental misunderstanding of the process of working with an architect can foil this essential collaboration at its genesis. A client who does not have a clear understanding of his or her own goals for a project may also experience disappointment.

In my own practice, we consider our clients to be an integral and inseparable part of the planning, design, and delivery of projects. We endeavor to maintain intimate and active communication with clients from project conception to completion. We address their particular objectives and constraints while providing them with new insight into the value of carefully considered and executed design solutions. Beyond this essential commitment to communication, we habitually craft a comprehensive and carefully detailed set of drawings and specifications commensurate with the craft and beauty we endeavor to achieve in our design solutions. This documentation is supported throughout the construction work by way of our assiduous administration of the construction contract.

The Return on Your Investment

An early client, who is now my dear friend, struggled during our preliminary discussions to understand what he perceived to be the excessive cost of our services. He presented his case by using simple math to show how many additional hours he would have to work to pay our fee. I responded in part with this letter:

While I must respect your ultimate decision, I would encourage you to more fully consider the potential of the arrangement we have discussed.

To measure the success of our proposed endeavor in terms of additional work for you fails to acknowledge the great value of what is sure to come of our effort together.

Were I a betting man, I would feel safe to wager that you will invest everything you can in pursuit of crafting the home you so earnestly desire. If this proves true, as I have come to expect as a benefit of my experience, you may well incur the additional investment regardless of whether you proceed with me or another—the marked distinction will become evident only in the result.

Accepting this as true for the sake of this argument, would you not be better to come out with something beautiful that will exceed your expectations, rather than something that is all but certain to fall short? I would argue, too, that the benefits of crafting your house into an essentially beautiful home will more than compensate for the anticipated cost to you.

A successful relationship with your architect will yield more for your life than you could ever measure by the investment of money or hours. My client came to appreciate this value as we proceeded together to craft his house into his ideal home.

Our modern world offers much to deplete our energies but little to restore them. At their essence, the best homes, conceived out of those special relationships in which owner and architect are in concert together, afford a sense of sanctuary within a circumstance of beauty and become a grace upon the landscape.

The client, architect, and cabinetmaker collaborated extensively on this kitchen remodel to create cabinets and case-work evocative of the original Arts and Crafts furniture in the client's home.

Resources

Architects

American Architects Directory
www.architects-in-america.com

The American Institute of Architects (AIA)
1735 New York Ave., NW
Washington, DC 20006-5292
202.626.7300
www.aia.org

American Institute of Building Design
2505 Main St., Ste. 209B
Stratford, Connecticut 06615
800.366.2423
www.aibd.org

American Society of Landscape Architects
636 Eye St., NW
Washington, DC 20001-3736
202.898.2444
www.asla.org

Architects USA Directory
www.architectsusa.com

Community Design Center of Pittsburgh (RIN)
Bruno Building
945 Liberty Ave., Loft #2
Pittsburgh, PA 15222
412.391.4144
www.cdcp.org

Gerald Lee Morosco Architects, P.C.
1819 East Carson St.
Pittsburgh, PA 15203
412.431.4347
www.glm-architects.com

National Council of Architectural Registration
  Boards (NCARB)
www.ncarb.org/stateboards/index.html

Construction

Building Online
www.buildingonline.com

Building Trades Directory
www.architecture.about.com

Guide to Construction Estimating
www.construction-guide.com

National Association of Homebuilders
1201—15th St., NW
Washington, DC 20005
800.368.5242
www.nahb.org

Urban Land Institute
1025 Thomas Jefferson St., NW
Ste. 500 West
Washington, DC 20007
202.624.7000
www.uli.org

Contractors
Contractors.com
www.contractors.com

ContractorsWebGuide.com
www.contractorswebguide.com

Home Contractors and Home Builders Online
www.localhomecontractors.com

ImproveNet
www.improvenet.com

ServiceMagic
www.servicemagic.com

Frank Lloyd Wright Projects and Resources
Fallingwater
www.paconserve.org/fw-about.asp

Frank Lloyd Wright Building Conservancy
www.savewright.org

Frank Lloyd Wright Foundation
www.franklloydwright.org

Frank Lloyd Wright Preservation Trust
www.wrightplus.org

Frank Lloyd Wright School of Architecture
www.taliesin.edu

Taliesin Preservation, Inc.
www.taliesinpreservation.org

Remodeling and Home Improvement
Energy Efficient Rehab Advisor
www.rehabadvisor.com

Home Building.com
www.homebuilding.com

HouseNet
www.housenet.com

National Association of the
  Remodeling Industry
780 Lee St., Ste. 200
Des Plaines, IL 60016
800.611.6274
www.nari.org

Old House Journal
www.oldhousejournal.com

The Old House Web
www.oldhouseweb.com

Remodeling Price Quotes
www.remodelingpricequotes.com

Workshops, Seminars, and Trade Shows
The Construction Expo
www.construction-expo.com

Grove Park Inn Arts and Crafts Conference
www.webteek.com/arts-craftsconference

The International Builders Show and tecHOMExpo
www.nahbexpos.com/Home

International Trade Show for Kitchen and Bath
www.ish-na.com

Southern Homebuilding Seminars
www.shbshome.com

Resources

Index